HOW A FRAGMENTED FAMILY
FOUND GOD AND EACH OTHER,
AND HOW YOU CAN TOO.

COME to the QUIET

THE STORY **ESCAPE TO GOD** LEFT OUT

JIM HOHNBERGER
WITH TIM & JULIE CANUTESON

Pacific Press® Publishing Association
Nampa, Idaho
Oshawa, Ontario, Canada
www.pacificpress.com

Designed by Linda Griffith
Cover art by Lars Justinen

Copyright © 2004 by
Pacific Press® Publishing Association
Printed in United States of America
All Rights Reserved

Additional copies of this book are available by calling toll free 1-800-765-6955 or
visiting http://www.adventistbookcenter.com.

ISBN: 0-1863-2032-2

04 05 06 07 08 • 5 4 3 2 1

DEDICATION

For all of those who find themselves busier and busier, yet accomplishing less and less; for all who are inundated with phone calls, emails, meetings, or the expectations of others; for any who are tired of the cares of life and the endless list of things to do, God is calling you to come to the quiet, not just to come to a quiet setting, but to come to the quiet of resting in Him. If you long to respond to His call, this book is dedicated to you.

It's also dedicated to our dear North Fork Valley and all of its inhabitants. You folks, both animal and human, as well as the river, the meadows, and mountains, were not only our nursery where we grew up into the Christian life but also our teachers. We thank you, dear friends, and while the valley we love so much has been drastically changed this year, and its glorious tranquility so terribly scarred, I pray that all may still catch a glimpse of your beauty once again in the pages of this book.

Other books by
Jim Hohnberger:

Escape to God
Empowered Living
It's About People

CONTENTS

FOREWORD

RANDY MAXWELL

God's sense of timing and sense of humor never cease to amaze me. Here I am writing the foreword to a book about slowing down and coming to "the quiet" at a time when, once again, I've said Yes too often, and the pressures of work, ministry, and home have pushed any sense of quiet far into the background.

My life is composed of deadlines. I'm in advertising—a stomach-acid-producing job that thrives on emergencies, "drop-dead" dates, and multi-tasking. I also have a family of five and a writing/speaking ministry that takes me all over the United States and beyond. Nerves get frayed. Relationships get shortchanged. Time with God gets clipped. And soon I have that sinking, yet familiar feeling of being out of control—that feeling of life leading me by the nose, jerking me here and there, from one crisis to another.

And that's why I'm glad for God's timing and His love of a good joke. Because in preparation to write Jim's foreword, I had to read his book. And in reading his book, I heard God's still, small voice gently reminding me to "be still, and know that [He is] God (Psalm 46:10)." If you identify with what I've just described and your life has become one big panic button that is being pushed by everyone and every thing else, you need this book.

I've known Jim and Sally for years as we've worked together getting covers developed for their books and tapes. They have mentored and prayed with me, and I feel I know their hearts. One thing I love and respect about this couple is their ability to uphold and live a high Christian standard without losing their grip on grace. They don't use their own lifestyle as a club of condemnation to bludgeon those who have a different experience. And by God's grace they've managed to avoid the legalistic pitfalls that have tripped up so many others.

Rather, they use the experiences God has given them—experiences in reprioritizing their lives, experiences in rekindling the spark in their marriage, experiences in bringing up children without the artificial stimulus of a material- and entertainment-crazed world, and experiences in self-surrender—to make us long for life beyond the treadmill. And more than this, they show us how to make it happen right where we live, whether that happens to be in a congested metropolis or in the country.

I commend this book to you. I've read it and heard God's call to come to the quiet—again. Now it's your turn. Let's listen while we still can.

Randy Maxwell
Nampa, Idaho
January 2004

Preface

Tim Canuteson

It was one of those beautiful days that makes one just enjoy living, a glorious afternoon that was going to be spoiled for me in a few short hours by the demands of my hospital job, but thankfully, it was the last day before vacation. One last errand remained to be completed before I would head into work, and that was to drive over to the small mall in town and pick up a special-order book that had come in. I lived in a wealthy area, and if it wasn't for the fact that I lived in hospital-subsidized housing, there would have been no way a young single guy like me could have afforded the rent.

The drive through town took me past brand-new office buildings and restored old homes—now worth millions. It was lunch hour, and the little town of 20,000 had a daytime population of 200,000 as the office parks filled up with workers. Well-dressed people out for their midday breaks filled the streets. Fashionably dressed women poured out of office buildings, and everywhere the scent of perfume and the feminine presence of wispy silks, of ribbons, of ruffles, and pearls wafted through the air. This peaceful and pleasant urban sight provided no hints of what was about to happen for the milling throngs who witnessed it. The traffic was bad and getting worse, but I was lucky enough to get a good parking spot, and I strolled casually into the bookstore to pick up my order.

Unknown to me, down at the other end of the mall, a beautiful young woman who worked at the jewelry store was taking her lunch break and, just like me, was planning to do errands. She got to her sports car just about the time I got back to my van. I backed out of my space, which was eagerly snatched by another busy shopper.

As I inched along in traffic, I saw this same young woman drive by in front of me. She had to slam on her brakes and stop suddenly as a car poked its nose out into her lane from the next row. Her body language was so expressive, it caught my eye. This lovely young woman was nearly in tears about this little problem. She threw up her hands in agitation, and thankfully, the older-looking woman in the passenger seat turned her head covered with long dirty blond hair and calmly directed the girl with her hands how to slightly pull out and go around the driver who had borrowed part of her lane with his car's nose. It almost looked like a driving lesson, and the young woman's white sports car continued down the road.

The impression left on me was strong, and I remember saying to myself, "Wow! Living here really stresses some people out. Poor girl!" That was nearly twenty years ago, and I can still see the whole scene vividly. The society we live in has only gotten worse, not better. We are increasingly stressed, pushed, and pressured. There has never been a time in history when we have had to make so many choices, about so many things, so fast, with so little thought, and with such long-lasting consequences.

Every day we are bombarded with decisions that just didn't exist years ago. What we wear is a good example. In olden times, you might have had only one real outfit. Not a lot of choice when it came time to get dressed. If you were fortunate, you had a set of good clothes and a set of everyday clothes. You ate the same food day in and day out and did the same activities every day for years on end in an endless routine very much like your parents before you and their parents before them. The opportunity to live in this era of history is precious, but it also comes with a very high price, and that price is reflected in a modern American longing for a simpler, quieter way of life. The appeal is nearly universal, as the success of *The Wilderness Family* and similar movies and TV programs have demonstrated.

Companies renowned for offering lifelong employment started to lay off employees, and loyalty to and respect for the employee became items unaffordable in the global economy. Health problems we have never faced in any great quantity have become epidemic thanks to pollution, lifestyle, and diet. Even free time is no longer "free" as constant communication is now available. Thoughts about God come hard in such a setting and soon are relegated to something that happens in church for a couple of hours once a week—if we are not too tired to get up and go, that is. Stresses come upon us every day from so many different directions that pretty soon we are like that poor young woman, frustrated and upset to the point of tears about what is happening to us.

Jim and Sally Hohnberger know all about life's stresses. About the very time I saw that young woman in the parking lot, they were moving their young family to the wilderness of the North Fork River Valley next door to Glacier National Park. They came to find the quiet, to find each other, and to find God. The quiet has transformed their lives, and through them has changed countless others, including mine. Years later, Jim had become a successful realtor, and he wrote an advertisement inviting people to "Come to the Quiet." Everyone who previewed the ad said it was terrible. "Who'd relate to such a silly idea?" they questioned, but Jim didn't agree and ran it anyway. The results spoke for themselves, for it seemed that *everyone* related to the desire to "come to the quiet."

My family and I spent ten days with Jim and Sally in late spring this year at their home in the North Fork Valley while roughing out this book. I can attest to the beauty of the wilderness, the peacefulness of the setting, and the rugged grandeur of the Rocky Mountains rising to the east, which continually draw one's thoughts heavenward. But as we worked and laughed about the incidents of the past and planned the book you hold in your hands, there is a young woman never too far removed from my thoughts, someone who can never be reached with this message, and someone who can never respond to the call of the quiet because she lingered too long somewhere else.

I went to work that day so very long ago and then left on vacation. I had no idea until I returned that the woman I had seen so upset was on the way to her death. I recognized her picture on the front page of the paper. The other woman with the dirty blond hair that I had seen was actually a man who had abducted her. He brutally murdered her and then dumped her poor abused body in a wooded area, taking her money, her car, her virtue, and her future. With her car and credit cards, he went on a wild spending spree that extended over several states before his eventual capture. That young woman drove past scores of people, just like me, who could have helped her if only we had known, but by the time we did, it was too late.

You, too, have those whom you can rescue from certain destruction if, and only if, you sense their danger and take the steps to protect them. If you are waiting for them to cry out, to tell you that they are in trouble, if you are waiting until they are in the clutches of the enemy, it may very well be too late, their cries for help too easily confused with something else. I watched one person on their way to certain death and never realized it at the time. The experience left me with a determination to never again allow a soul to slip by on the way to destruction.

Within your heart and mind lives the desire to live as God designed us to—in communion with Him. Communion with God is not easily found at the speed most of us are traveling through our days, and yet, if you will listen, His still, small voice is faintly calling us to the quiet of His presence to meet with Him. Some can respond to his call at once, while others may have to work to free up the time to visit with Him, while still others may not find the God they seek unless they totally change their life and location. I can't tell you what God will ask of you, but I can assure you it is for your very best. All are called to come to the quiet. You may come to the quiet by moving to the wilderness, or you may find it in the quiet of your room, in a crowded bus, or even in a jail cell. Coming is what matters; so come. God is calling you now, and like that young woman, none of us know which day may be our last. Come now, before it is forever too late!

CHAPTER 1

OFF THE TREADMILL

Oh LORD, I know that the way of man is not in himself: it is not in man that walketh to direct his steps (Jeremiah 10:23).

All alone with God, I was perched on a wilderness cliff at 7,100 feet, overlooking several small lakes gleaming in the valley below. My Bible lay idly on my lap as I reflected on a passage I had just read in the book of Jeremiah. "O LORD, I know that the way of man is not in himself: it is not in man that walketh to direct his steps" (10:23). *What does this mean?* I pondered. *How does this apply to my life? How can it be?* After all, I had run my own affairs for thirty years before I came to know God. *Lord, what do You mean, the way of man is not in himself?* The beautiful scene around me faded as, in my mind's eye, I looked back in time and God took me on a walk through all the chapters of my life to the present. Hours passed unnoticed.

Perhaps before going any further I had better tell you how I came to be on this remote ledge.

The boundary between the western United States and Canada is arbitrary, following no geological features, so when I moved to northern Montana I found that the Whitefish Mountain range in the United States is suddenly the Macdonald Range in British Columbia. Likewise, the Flathead River, which drains much of southeastern British Columbia, transforms itself into the North Fork of the Flathead River after crossing the U.S. border. The names change, but the mountains and rivers remain the same, little knowing or caring what puny men say about them.

Today this valley is referred to as the Trans-Boundary Flathead Area, and it is one of the most scenic, unsettled, and special places left in the interior of North America. Yet human beings have exploited its timber, its valuable minerals, and its oil. Its lush growth has nurtured countless grazing animals over the years, and still the area remains surprisingly unchanged compared to areas people have abused and exploited for short-term gain. It is an extraordinarily vibrant place, supporting with few exceptions the same basic ecosystem and wildlife that was there half a millennium ago. Only Yellowstone National Park can compare.

I will never forget the reaction Sally and I had when we first viewed this valley, which runs almost eighty miles roughly north and south, from Canada well into the United States. We had spent days looking for just the right place in which to escape from the rat race and make our home, and here it was. We gave each other the thumbs-up sign. We knew we had found our special place! Hemmed in by the Whitefish Mountains to the west and the Livingston Range in Glacier National Park to the east, the valley encompasses nearly 1,600 square miles, with almost a thousand of those in Montana. The river runs the length of the valley with no significant human development, and only one unincorporated settlement—Polebridge. The valley's year-round population once peaked back in the homestead days at about 150 before falling rapidly, and it never climbed again until recent years. Even ten years after we moved here, there remained just over eighty year-round residents in the U.S. section and none in the Canadian. Even with summer homes swelling the population by the hundreds, the numbers remain remarkably small.

But it was not always so. The Ktunaxa, called the Kootenay in Canada and Kootenai in the United States, were the Native American inhabitants whose names for many landmarks linger even to-day. This small nation once numbered nearly 10,000 until small-pox killed nine out of ten members in the eighteenth century.

Even in such an isolated and beautiful location, the pressures of modern life can get to be too much and crowd out those things that should be most important to us. I have found that unless I make a concerted effort to preserve it, I will not have the time to commune with God, and when that relationship suffers, all my other human relationships suffer too. One of the solutions I have found to depressurize my life even in such an idyllic setting is to take some time away from the rest of the world and just spend it alone with God in the wilderness. I refer to this time as my Enoch time, after the Bible character who walked with God, and it was for one of these times that I had planned this trip to Nasukoin Lake. ("Nasukoin" is the Ktunaxa word for chief.)

Parking near the trailhead on the remote gravel strip called Moose Creek Road, I shouldered my fifty-five–pound pack for the seven-mile trek. The area I chose to hike in is, geologically speaking, glaciated with long deep lakes, waterfalls, U-shaped valleys, and cliffs. If this sounds to you like a lot of work, you're right, because all 3,000 feet of it is uphill. The trail guides rate this hike as "strenuous." I consider it moderate, at least by my standards.

This area is a major grizzly corridor, so I set up my tent in a less likely bear area, amid some boulders overlooking a lake. I was alone with nothing but bears, mountain goats, marmots, squirrels, and God. I finished setting up camp, had my supper, and hung my food out of reach of the bears, then settled in for the night. Real quiet is something few people in our world today get to experience. As the sun set, my attention was drawn to the sounds of the forest. Just before sleep overtook me, I contemplated the morning and what it might hold, and decided to climb up above the valley the next day.

Summer mornings in the mountains can be chilly, and at a 6,600-foot elevation it was, but there are tradeoffs. The morning was glorious, with the still lake reflecting the majestic peaks that rose more than two thousand feet above me. As I climbed, a shrill whistle sounded high up on the ledges, and an enraged scream drew my gaze overhead, where a bald eagle noted the warning whistle of the marmots and with a graceful, effortless turn, headed down the valley, seeking less-alert prey.

Climbing out of the valley, I settled in on an exposed ledge about five hundred feet higher than my camp. The view was spectacular, and the sun was warming the rocks. I settled down there and took out my Bible, expecting to study, never anticipating what God had in store for me that day. This was the time when, as I contemplated my life, the world about me slowly faded away and I found myself reliving the past with a vividness that is nearly impossible to describe. It left an impression impossible to forget!

As I wandered back in time, I could hear my father say, "Look at him! Look at him! Isn't that odd?" Glancing into my family's kitchen, I could see old Dr. Hildebrand, the family doctor, clutching his worn black leather bag. In those days doctors still made house calls. He glanced at me, not even a toddler yet, and studied my actions over the top of his half-moon glasses. He smiled.

"Well, I'll be. That little fella sure does crawl backwards. Don't worry about it. I've seen it before, and it's usually a sign of a baby that just learned to do things differently. I'm sure he's bright enough in his own way."

"Isn't normal!" my father retorted, and they were both right. I have never been one to follow the "normal" or accepted paths of life without some difficulty. I was such a simple child with such a simple mind that many things others seem to take for granted baffled me. My father was a simple man who prospered with one great skill. He was a good worker, and dependable! Mated with my mother, who worked hard and also loved the simple daily routine of life, following the same pattern day after day for seemingly endless years, it is not surprising that little Jimmy Hohnberger, the middle child of five, turned out to be simple in taste and intellect.

Kindergarten was the very first time in my life that I was stretched beyond my comfort zone. Painfully shy, and I mean *painfully* shy, I was forced into a room with more children than I had seen in my life, and I hid under the teacher's desk. The kindly woman allowed this oddity, because she sensed how different I was and figured I would quickly come out of my shell. To her surprise I spent thirty days under her desk!

Finally she and my mother had a talk and decided the time had come for me to cease living as a caveman and come out. When they explained this to me, I was terrified. I couldn't face it, and when I was sent to school the next day, I played hooky. I was just a little fellow, but I stood in the park for what seemed forever, until at last I heard the school bell ring. Then I happily skipped home, thinking my ordeal was over. However, my mother was pretty smart and started asking me about my school day. When my answers didn't mesh, she quickly found out the truth; for you see, the bell I had heard was the noontime bell. I was never punished for this infraction, and for several days my mother came to school and helped me in the transition to life at a desk.

School to me was something I endured because I had to, but I never mixed well with the other children due to my shyness. I simply had no confidence in my opinions or abilities and hence made relatively few friends. I had no desire to study, to read for knowledge's sake, or to excel. Often I could not even comprehend the subject of study, but I was far too shy to seek help from the teachers. Rarely did my schoolbooks get opened, but I managed to consistently get C grades. I couldn't wait until school was over and I could seek freedom in the fields and woods.

Appleton, Wisconsin, is not exactly renowned for its forested areas, but I spent many hours happily playing among the trees and waterways of the local golf course. The golf course management did not approve of this activity, and the groundskeepers spent considerable time chasing me both on foot and in maintenance trucks. The faster they chased, the faster I ran. Exactly what would have happened if they caught me, I can't say, because they never did.

At eleven, I inherited my brother's paper route. You were supposed to be a minimum of twelve years old, but because they liked my brother, they let me have the job. This again forced me out of my comfort zone because I had to do collections, some monthly, some weekly, for ninety-five homes, which meant I had to talk to people—lots of them, and strangers at that. I was scared! Yet looking back, I can see it was part of God's plan to bring me out of my extreme shyness, and through that route I met some very nice people.

None had as much influence on me as Mrs. Barliment. She was completely crippled with arthritis that had left her body bent, twisted, and confined to a chair, but it didn't rob her of her smile nor her loving concern for others. She wanted me to bring her paper right into the house because of her condition, but she wasn't content just to have me drop it off. She always asked me questions and tried to draw me out. Somehow, in her presence, I didn't have to be so shy. After all, what could she do to me? Her efforts paid off, and we soon became fast friends. Within months I was working for her regularly, raking leaves, painting the house, and shoveling snow—whatever needed doing. She showed me that I *could* talk to adults.

I began work at the gas station as a high-school sophomore through my father's influence, washing cars for seventy-five cents an hour. My father passed his work ethic on to me, and soon I was promoted to pumping gas and performing minor mechanical procedures like oil changes and replacing water pumps and mufflers. Yet again this forced me to interact with people from all walks of life.

I endured the rest of high school, never studying or caring about my grades, which remained average at best. I had no confidence in my academic ability, but while I remained shy I could now talk to people, and somehow I matured into a blond young man with piercing bluish-green eyes. To my shock and delight, a number of lovely young ladies began making it known that they wanted to go out with me. I even got to date the homecoming queen!

In high school I wanted to take shop and build things. My mother had other ideas. She made up her mind that one of her sons was going to college, and I was the one. She insisted I take college prep courses. Because math came easily for me, they decided to place me in chemistry, which just about blew my poor little mind. There was one nice aspect about chemistry, and that was Sally Hughes, the pretty girl who sat behind me. God arranged things so I would come in contact with the one girl in the whole school who was perhaps even shier than I was. She would become, unbeknownst to me then, the love of my life.

The night before college entrance exams, I went out with my friends and had a few too many. My test scores were terrible, thanks to my hangover. College seemed completely out of reach. My father made too much money for me to get student aid and too little to pay my way. What would I study, anyway? The only thing I liked was the out-of-doors, and how do you get a degree in that?

I got a job in a paper and plastics company, but the union didn't like the work ethic my father had so faithfully instilled in me. The work was easy and boring. I could do my job and set up the work for the next couple of days or more. The union complained that I was too productive and doing more than anyone else. They moved me to a different section, and the same thing happened. At last, through my father's influence, I was moved to the company's "pounding out" section. My job involved using a sledgehammer to separate Cool Whip lids from the large sheets of plastic they were made from. Three days of this back-breaking work and I quit and went back to the gas station. I started thinking about college again, which was, of course, my father's and God's intention.

Interested at last, I found out that Michigan Technological University had a degree in forestry with a minor in surveying. The problem was that out-of-state tuition was $4,000 a semester. I couldn't afford that, but divine Providence had plans for me. One evening I was working at the station when a well-to-do gentleman came in. He walked in while I was filling up his luxury car—checking the tire pressure and the oil and washing the windows. As I worked, I was talking to a friend about how I hated factory work and couldn't afford the tuition up at Michigan Tech and just didn't know what I was going to do.

I didn't realize that the owner of the car had been listening to my story. Finally he turned and said, "Do you want to go to college?"

"Well, yeah. Why?" I replied uncertainly.

"Here's my address. Come and see me at my office Wednesday." With that he was gone.

It was all very mysterious. When I told my boss about the situation, he exclaimed, "Don't you know who that was? That was Mr. Bulboz, one of the richest men in town. He has his own insurance company. I don't know what he wants, but you had better get yourself down there on Wednesday."

It was with some trepidation that I showed up fresh from the service station, with a grease rag still hanging out of my back pocket. After I had been escorted into Mr. Bulboz's immaculate office, he began to ask me about myself. He especially wanted to know if I was religious. "I'm Catholic," I told him honestly, but he cut me off. He said he didn't care about the specifics, just wanted to know if I went to church. After a lengthy interview, he asked me how much I needed for tuition, and then he told me, "Go to college, son. Your bills will be paid."

"But—" I stammered.

He raised his hand, cutting me off again. "All I require is for you to maintain a B average and to promise that when you are able, you will help others as you have been helped." So I promised, and I was off to college. Once more God was ordering events beyond my ability to control.

Thanks to hard work, I did well in college. One significant problem was that I had to work as well as study just to keep a few dollars in my pocket. Even worse, Sally, my high-school sweetheart, was a few hundred miles away at her nursing school. People say that long-distance relationships don't work, but Sally and I didn't know that. We worked very hard every week and almost always made it home to see each other on the weekends. To me, it was worth all the extra study, all the hours on the road, and all the time working at the gas station, just to see her for a few hours Friday through Sunday.

One weekend at home, I went by my brother's place of employment to see him, but he wasn't in. He worked for a computer sales company, and since he was supposed to return shortly, I decided to wait. The grouping of open offices allowed almost everyone there to see what was happening throughout the office area, and when the boss looked out of his office and saw me, he invited me in to chat, just being friendly. He was engrossed with the computer in front of him, and it caught my interest. After all, this was 1972, and computers were not the common item we think of today. "Trying to figure out this surveying program," he commented by way of explanation. "Know anything about it?"

"Let me see what you're doing," I said, as I walked behind his desk. Within minutes I helped him solve his problem. I didn't know anything about computers, but I knew surveying, and suddenly the boss was offering me a job when I finished college, selling computers to surveyors.

Now keep in mind, at that point in my life I considered sales to be about the lowest profession there was. This was simply a reflection of my personality. I looked down on any profession that required someone to speak to strangers, and salesmen were the worst. Even being approached by a salesman made my palms sweat because they were essentially strangers who wanted to talk to me. So to my brother's boss I politely declined any commitment at that point. I told him my degree was in forestry, and I planned to seek employment within my own field.

Sally and I married in March of 1972 and graduated that same spring. Toward the end of my program I started looking for forestry positions, but the only ones that turned up were either temporary or didn't have much to do with forestry. One was as a department consultant teaching farmers how to plant more trees to provide habitat for pheasants. Another position offered to relocate me out of state for a temporary position cleaning park bathrooms! I wasn't very interested. Then a lumberyard owner offered me a sales job, thinking that I must know lumber because I had studied forests. Things were going from bad to worse.

On top of all this, Sally and I had gone out looking at new houses one weekend while we were home from college, just for a lark. We found a cute little place we liked a lot. I negotiated with the builder, not really serious, just showing off for my girl. I wanted to impress her with my great negotiating skills. Suddenly we reached the point where I had gotten everything we wanted, and the man pulled out a contract. I can't believe it now, but we signed it. We signed just before Sally started work as a nurse in our hometown.

The bank came back and told us that they would give us a loan only if I could prove I was employed. I really needed a job!

I finally swallowed my pride and went back to the computer company to see my brother's boss. The man was nearly in hysterics when he heard my story. "You bought a brand-new house without a job?" He laughed until tears came to his eyes. "Hohnberger," he continued, "you're going to be one great salesman because you're motivated." And so I was off to the world of sales, sucked in by circumstances, or so I thought at the time, little understanding how God operates. I know now that God placed me in the one profession I couldn't stand and wanted to have nothing to do with. Breaking into my thoughts as I sat on that sunny ledge, God said, *"Jim, I was preparing you for your real life work, wasn't I?"* He may have been, but I wasn't the greatest student.

Immediately the company sent me for thirty days of training in New York. I was a young kid just out of college, in classes with a bunch of middle-aged professional salesmen. I felt stupid and out of place, but I was motivated.

The trainers taught us how to make sales, how to present the product, and how to relate to the client. I really desired to succeed, to have a nice home, cars, to go places, to see and to do things, to make it in life, and to become somebody. Unwittingly I had taken my first step onto the treadmill of life, and it forced me to travel for training. Thirty days away from my Sally. This was longer than we had spent apart in four years of college. Yet, I had been sold on the idea that I was investing in our future. I came home determined to provide everything Sally ever needed or even longed for materially.

And I sold nothing—not one single thing! Six months went by, and I had still sold *nothing!* I tried and tried to do just what I had been taught and got nowhere. Worse, Sally had to carry the load of providing for us, working as a registered nurse. She never complained, but my self-esteem plummeted lower and lower. I was a man, and to me, a man provided for his family. At last, in desperation, I decided to throw away all that I had been taught and do it my way. I was going to just be Jim, and if the client didn't like it, well, I couldn't do any worse than I was right now.

The company had just introduced a new accounting program, so I went to see a certified public accountant to whom my racquetball partner referred me. I asked if I could input his data into our system for one day. By the end of the day he saw what the system could do for him, and he was sold on the product.

Now knowing that presenting my computer systems in a practical way worked better, I went into a company and asked the boss if I could spend the day with the people who would actually use the system. He said, "Sure." So I showed them my system and what it could do for them, and they *loved* it. They insisted the company buy the computers, and I walked out with the biggest contract my company had ever received. I quit trying to "sell" the bosses and just worked with the staff.

My new approach was a great success, and orders flowed in. I started expanding the market for our systems to other businesses, and they loved them too. I would let potential clients use our system for thirty days, and afterwards they almost always bought. Everything was going great. My boss was delighted with my sales after waiting so long for me to catch on.

But soon he grew tired of paying out so much money to me in commission. He started playing around with my commission structure so my cut would be smaller, not just once, but twice. After the second time, I decided to confront him. I pointed my finger right at him and declared, "You're cheating me!"

His face got red, and he half rose from his chair, "Don't you accuse me of that again!" he retorted.

"You are cheating me!" I repeated again, "and you have given me a lot to think about on vacation." I finished and walked out of his office. While on vacation, I made up my mind that I would never work for somebody else again. Now I had to find a business I could run on my own.

I looked at several business opportunities, but one insurance company really made a strong pitch. I was resistant. If being a salesman was the lowest profession in my mind, insurance sales were the lowest of the low. However, I checked them out and found that this particular company held the vast majority of policies in Wisconsin. Maybe it wouldn't be so bad representing a winning company in my own business. Thus began the Hohnberger Agency, and I quickly made my little start-up agency into a productive business.

Having to start my own business set us back six months.

When our firstborn, Matthew, was born, Sally stopped working as a nurse at the time we could least afford it. This added an additional burden of both the income loss and the new little life depending upon me to provide for it.

But soon prosperity returned, and with it came better cars and a larger home. We developed an active social life with friends and family, but the pace of life began to increase from sunup to sundown—traffic on the roads, sports at the racquet club, golf every Sunday morning, the caring for my firstborn child—and these stresses all started to affect the one thing that had really mattered to us in all of our poor years—our relationships with each other.

When we were dating, Sally was everything to me. She was, quite literally, the one thing I lived for, and yet now, after just a short time, she was no longer my entire life. She became a convenience: She was nice to have, she met some of my needs, but she no longer held that special place of being all that I needed or ever wanted.

The stresses of life were slowly adding up and had their effect on my mind and body. I was a businessman and had to deal with payrolls, taxes, employee problems, unprofitable accounts, and the stress of living the modern life with its never-ending phone calls and messages. The worst part was the stress of knowing somewhere deep inside, on an intuitive level, that things were just not what they should be, that my career was robbing me, running me, controlling me, rather than me controlling it. Yet I was baffled. How to handle the problem I faced? What else could I do? I was supposedly living the American dream, with a business and an income most people only dream about. I could still put on a cheerful face in public, but at home, where I felt I could be myself, I was tired and irritable.

We had friends who moved from the Midwest to Miami, and they wrote a letter about their new home. It ran like this:

Dear Jim and Sally,
Miami is something else. Even now the traffic is terrible. Later it will be even worse. Lots of accidents. Papers are loaded with every kind of misdemeanor, drugs, political corruption, murders, and other unspeakable crimes. It's bad, bad and seems worse because everything is made public. Nothing is hushed up. In Wisconsin, there was as much or more, but you only hear half of what's going on. That's what is amazing here. Police sirens, helicopters all day long, really weird, but I'm getting used to it. Even with security, it is a testy deal not only at night, but in the daylight. But I'm getting used to it.

Driving to my office in rush-hour traffic, gagging on the exhaust from the bus in front of me, I thought about my friend's letter, and I began to wonder about my life and what it was gaining us. Sure Appleton, Wisconsin, is not as bad as Miami, but I longed for the quiet. We had recently become Christians, after one of my clients introduced us to the Bible, and I noticed with interest some Bible characters I had never read about. I had always thought the Bible was a collection of fairy tales and prayers. Now I was discovering it was full of people like Enoch, a man who walked with God during his life on earth. This fascinated me. I wanted to walk with God like that, wanted to have just that type of intimate relationship with Him. If God would do it with Enoch, why wouldn't He walk with me in the same way? Yet I didn't find anyone in the church who could really tell me how to do that.

I also longed to do special things and recapture the magic of our marriage. Sally suggested that this is what people do when they retire, so I started talking with businessmen I knew who either had retired or were getting closer to retirement. Boy, was I shocked! These men no longer liked or hardly knew their wives—if they were still married at all. Many of them were on the second or third marriage by that point. Was this all the future held for us, material success at the price of all that should make life worthwhile?

Arriving at my office, I found a letter from the insurance company informing me that because of my great sales record I was being awarded an all-expenses-paid trip for two to Reno, Nevada. I didn't gamble and didn't feel that gambling was acceptable for a Christian. However, looking at the map, I saw Yosemite National Park was within easy driving distance of Reno. "Come on, Sally, let's go to Reno," I said, "and we'll just go to Yosemite instead of the casinos." That's what we did, and for the first time in our lives caught a vision of what the mountains held and how humanity was really intended to live in nature and close to nature's God.

We tasted of the quiet, and God seemed to draw very near us in that place. I felt tension drain away that I didn't even know I had, and in its place the beginnings of the peace and rest I had longed for. I realized that my life was a lot like the treadmill I exercised on. At four miles an hour I can think or talk. I can do it at five, six, or seven miles an hour. But when I get it up to eleven miles per hour, I can't think, can't talk, can hardly hear what anyone is saying. All I can do is barely hang on and run. It gave me a good picture of the life I was leading. I was so busy that I couldn't think about God, hear Him speak to me, or take time to speak to Him. I had even less time for Sally and the children.

Sally and I determined to change all that, and we ended up taking a course of action that led us to sell our home, cars, and most of our possessions. It left us misunderstood by nearly everyone we knew, and it would forever change the course of our lives and our understanding about God. It would lead us through a chain of God-led events to start sharing our story with a world that is still on the treadmill of life and just barely hanging on.

I could never have planned out or charted the course of my life, and here on this ledge God spent hours reviewing with me all that had transpired. *"My hand guided you, though you knew Me not. I loved you and directed your life, and it has not been your own. I ordered your steps, and I will direct your future,"* God told me after He showed to me the entire scope of my life and explained how each circumstance, difficulty, and victory was part of His plan to bring me to where I am today. There was nothing I could say. In awed silence, I contemplated how God had led me step by step.

Slowly I realized I was not alone on the ledge. I had heard animal and bird noises all day, but only now, as that wonderful communion with God was ending, did I pay any attention to them. I opened my eyes to the unblinking stare of a vulturelike bird hesitantly hopping toward me. Seeing my eyes open, he cocked his head as if evaluating how weak I was. Without moving my head I glanced to my left; the trees were full of scavengers. I moved my eyes right; several more waited in the trees over there. Gazing upward, I saw more creatures circling, all waiting for the moment when they could confirm my death and enjoy a wilderness feast. *How long have I been here,* I wondered? I lifted my head slightly to consider the boldest bird, still looking as if he'd like to give me a good peck.

"Get out of here," I hollered as I rose and shook myself. The sky filled with flapping wings. "I'm not dead yet," I said, still talking out loud to those old buzzards. I had come to the wilderness to seek something, and those birds were not completely wrong that day. I had no idea what God had to show me when I came to the quiet, but I found I had to die to all that I was, all that I wanted, all that I ever hoped to be. "Yes, birds, you were studying a dead body, but you didn't know it."

I had to die so God could raise me up in newness of life and purpose. He awaits the opportunity to do the same for you, and all He requires is your willingness. God took me on a journey that covered fifty years of my life without me moving a muscle, and He can take you to the quiet of His presence, even if you never set foot in the wilderness. So come. Come to God. Come and have the deepest needs of your soul satisfied. Come to the quiet.

CHAPTER 2

DOWNSIZING

A little that a righteous man hath is better than the riches
of many wicked (Psalm 37:16).

Companies in trouble have always laid people off, and if you were affected by such action, you were fired, laid off, or let go. In the last couple of decades, such brutal terms have been replaced with a new and somewhat nebulous term—downsizing. Companies downsize to save money and increase the profit margin, and workers nowadays complain that they were downsized. I suppose that it is less painful to admit to being downsized than to simply admit you were terminated because you did not serve a useful and profitable purpose for the company.

As hard as downsizing may be for those affected, in most cases it does achieve what the company desires in creating a leaner and more efficient operation. Sometimes entire departments are simply eliminated along with their product lines. This may be drastic action, but when the current organizational structure isn't obtaining the goals that the owners desire, it is time for reorganization.

Every one of us, whether we realize it or not, is running our own business in life, and if we run a business as our employment we must realize that this is simply the profit-making division of our larger corporation. J. W. Hohnberger and Company had all the requirements of a typical company, and yet business practices I would never have tolerated in my insurance agency were accepted and tolerated in the larger and more important company that my household comprised. When I started prayerfully considering the situation in which Sally and I found ourselves, some interesting concepts became clear to me, and I have learned to thank God for His insights.

The very first thing God made clear to me was to *get out of debt*. He wanted me to clear up our mortgage, our car loans, our student loans, and our credit cards. He made me understand that "the borrower is servant to the lender" (Proverbs 22:7). Sally and I had done very well by worldly standards, with all the toys and trappings of success, and yet when we added it all up, seventy five percent of our earnings went in one form or another to a banker we owed money to. Our God wants us to owe no person anything.

I've heard people say they would just walk away from their debts and everything else if times got tough, and while I do not doubt their sincerity, I do doubt their understanding of the situation. Debt controls us. It controls our time and our focus, and if we will not break its hold upon us when things are relatively easy, then we will not do so when things are harder. So what do we do?

Sally and I wanted financial freedom, so we started by reducing the load we were carrying. It is kind of like the pioneers who headed west in their covered wagons. They had with them only what they thought was the bare minimum of belongings and supplies. Yet, if there was some misfortune, if they lost too many oxen or the way turned out to be harder than anticipated, they started throwing out their treasures along the trail. We sold my Jeep with its plow and my large John Deere tractor. We stopped spending money to eat out. We had plans to buy a little cottage as a second home and a Corvette, both of which were eliminated. As we were able, we increased our payments on our other debts.

We started the process with things we could see were excessive and let the Lord lead us to other things that at first we probably would have never picked out as something that needed to be sold or eliminated. This is important, for the process of change is gradual, and we are doing God's will for us when we start on what we know He is asking us to do. More light and wisdom come as we live up to the knowledge we already have. This process continued until we had one used vehicle and the smallest home we had ever lived in.

Yet there is more to downsizing than just cost cutting. I have a friend who worked for a big company that got into money trouble a few years ago. Interestingly, he told me the core business was doing great—good productivity and huge contracts. "Well, how did you get in trouble?" I asked him.

"We got distracted. It was just that simple. You see, the company felt they had this great business that generated fantastic cash flow, but the market was saturated, and we couldn't expect big returns. Growth at a few percent a year just wasn't good enough for the guys at the top, so they got us involved in real estate, in golf courses, in retail stores, and in providing extras like Internet service and Web design. We were chasing pennies under the table in these other businesses, and when the economy turned down, as it always does sooner or later, these businesses that none of us really knew or understood just dragged us down with them. The shareholders were not happy. They sacked most of the senior leadership and brought in new people, who sold off all the extras and got us focused on our core business again. It will take a couple of years, but we will be profitable again thanks to regaining our focus."

I could relate to this because in a personal sense Sally and I had to go through the same thing. I read what Paul wrote in 1 Corinthians 2:2. "For I determined not to know any thing among you, save Jesus Christ, and him crucified." When we looked at our life, this was not the case. There were lots of artificial things distracting us from our heart's desire to really know Jesus Christ. The television consumed hours every week, and little if anything I watched had significant value. The newspaper took up more time to tell me in detail what I had already heard on the TV news, and magazines did about the same. All of them kept us from the best, from knowing God and being a family, which, when I considered it, was what I wanted more than comedies or depressing news.

I loved sports. I liked to play them, loved to watch them. I grew up in Green Bay Packer territory, and every Sunday found me watching at least one game. Have you any idea how much time that is? At least three hours, six if I watched two games. And then there was Monday Night Football, which kept me up some nights until almost midnight.

Of course, with all these other things taking up my time, I rarely took the time to talk, I mean really talk, with Sally. Without my interest, she had to have some outlet, so she spent hours on the telephone talking to her friends or going to the shopping malls.

These things were all distractions, and we decided to cut them out. We found we had a lot more time to visit with each other, to spend time with our children. Our home became happier.

As we started to enjoy each other once more, together we began looking at the other areas of life. There were weeks we had some type of social obligation almost every night of the week. We like people and enjoyed getting together, but we decided to cut our time spent this way in half. Church offices and various board meetings came under the same scrutiny, and we decided God would have us cut back even on some of the things we did at church when our motivation was to find Him and to bring our family into harmony with His principles.

God is never satisfied unless He is providing us the very best, and He knew that with my schedule I had no time to exercise, so when we changed our commitments He encouraged me to start exercising and to stop snacking. When I did, the twenty extra pounds I had gained came off. Sally and I started walking and running together.

We found that our time was all our children really desired. But among all the changes, the most remarkable were the changes in me.

I was happier, less irritable, and had found hope that our marriage could become the wonderful romantic relationship it had once been.

Coming to the quiet isn't just a change of address. We began to make these changes before we ever moved, before we even thought of moving. What had changed was our heart's desires and focus. When we altered that, our whole life's direction was affected.

If you already live in a quiet setting, you can take many of the steps needed to obtain most of the benefits of coming to the quiet without moving. That's how we began. We began where we were, on a beautiful country property in a large log home. So why didn't we just stay where we were? Our large country home had an equally large mortgage, and even though we had cut back and downsized, the long hours I had to work to pay that mortgage still robbed me of the time I needed for God, for Sally, and my precious boys. One of the primary motivations for moving to the Northwest was our desire to free up more of my time. The important thing to understand is that we started the process right where we were and gained many, many benefits prior to moving.

When we began to do things differently and reprioritize our lives, there was a certain backlash from our friends, our families, and our fellow church members. People started talking about us, and while we understood that in many cases the motivation was concern for us, we quickly found that people started relating to us differently than they had before. We understand now that when you do things outside of the normal expectations of society, people are going to treat you accordingly. But at the time, it hurt us when friends and family didn't understand.

Many of us live amid a sea of things. Sally and I did, and as I have traveled the globe and stayed in countless homes, I can affirm that many others do too. For example, I saw one woman's closet with fifty pairs of shoes! Another couple, when showing me their walk-in closet, gave me permission to count. I counted thirty dresses, thirty-nine blouses, thirty-five skirts. I gave up on her husband's side after finding forty-nine ties. A teenager we met had twenty-five pairs of brand-name tennis shoes. In another home a man was receiving fifty magazine subscriptions. One family had a home so packed that when we arrived there wasn't a free spot to put down our luggage or to hang our clothes. This made an impression on these dear folk, and they started a bonfire with their excess things and kept it burning for two days! I have known people to build additions on their homes just to get increased storage space. It has been said that one family might survive on the excess of another, and in some cases it might just be true!

We laugh at these extreme examples, but we don't have to look far to find the things that hold *us* in bondage. Thankfully we don't have to remain this way, if we are willing to put forth the effort it will take to break out of the patterns we have established. Downsizing can be for you, as it was for us, a joy that will help bring new focus and new vitality to your life. It might lead you to a country setting or even the wilderness. It is certain that if you downsize under heaven's supervision, you will find your steps tending upward and the things of this life losing their appeal. That this would be your experience is my prayer and my heart's desire for you. I'd like to leave you with a poem that probably says it better than I ever can.

Things! Things! Things!
On the table, on the floor,
Tucked away behind the door;
On the shelves and on the chairs:
Dangerously on the stairs.
Bureaus crammed and closets filled,
Boxes packed and boxes spilled:
Bundles everywhere you go,
Heaps and piles that overflow
Of Things! Things! Things!

Things! Things! Things!
Things of value, worthless trash;
Things preserved or gone to smash,
Ancient things and things just bought,
Common things and things far sought.
Things you mean to throw away,
Things you hope to use some day:
Cellar, attic, all between
One exasperating scene
Of Things! Things! Things!

Things! Things! Things!
Things that take our precious time;
Hold us from the life sublime,
Things that only gather dust,
Things that rot and things that rust;
Things that mold and things that freeze:
Things that harbor foul disease,
Things that mock us and defy,
Till at last we grimly die
Of Things! Things! Things!

Things! Things! Things!
Let me cease to be their fool,
Let me fly their crafty rule!
Let me with unsparing knife
Cut their canker from my life!
Broad and clear and all serene
Let me make my mansion clean
From Things! Things! Things!
                    —Amos R. Wells

CHAPTER 3

MULTITUDE TO THE MOUNTAIN

My people shall dwell in a peaceable habitation, and in sure
dwellings, and in quiet resting places (Isaiah 32:18).

Sally and I had lived our whole lives amid the multitudes—not in the *big* city, but where the pressures of modern society were always upon us. Even when we moved out of the city to a beautiful forty-acre property, we were still surrounded by the multitudes. Living in the city brings with it a number of pressures and concerns that weigh a person down, like an extra burden they must carry. And yet one can live in the suburbs or even in the country and bring the city lifestyle there.

Multitudes can be more than just people; they can be a multitude of tasks, a multitude of jobs, a multitude of responsibilities, a multitude of obligations, a multitude of expectations, a multitude of debts, or even just the multitudinous complexity of the life many of us have adopted. Living the city life is hard in the city, but there is something even worse, and that is trying to live the city life in the country, where the convenience of services and stores are not just a block or two away.

We know. We tried it, and it doesn't work very well. Of all the things that modern life robs from us, the most difficult for us to deal with is the loss of time, and time is our most limited commodity. The city life in the country robs you of even more time than it does in the city. Do you feel time-pressured like we did?

There was never enough time to do the things we really wanted to do, not even enough time to always do the things we *needed* to do. And the one area that got consistently shortchanged to make up the difference was the time available to spend with God, with each other as a couple, and as a family.

We moved to the mountains to escape from the time pressures, but with some careful thought and foresight, such drastic action may not be needed. You must remember we left for the mountains not because we had a well-thought-out plan of what we were going to accomplish but in the absence of such a plan. There were no books like the one you hold in your hands to show us the experience of others, so we laid our plans, by and large, in the dark. The Lord was very merciful to us in that things worked out as well as they did, and by no means do I think that everyone must follow our pathway to success in the Christian life. However, all must, in their own way, find the quietness of God's presence if they want to be Christians in anything more than name only.

It is hard to fully understand if you have never experienced it, but here in the mountains, in this last pristine valley of American wilderness, there was beauty everywhere we looked—no billboards, no stoplights, no traffic, no power lines, not even any telephones. Here, we are as likely to cross paths with a bear or a moose when we walk down the road as we are another person. A walk in the park (Glacier National Park) took on a whole new meaning. Instead of manicured lawns and swing sets, it was mountain lions, elk, mountain goats, and even the wolverine or lynx that we would see.

In place of trying to keep our children from playing with or stepping in someone's thoughtlessly discarded chewing gum, we could let them bend down and drink out of the streams and springs. Adventures unlimited awaited us, only requiring that we step into and experience them by hiking, canoeing, or backpacking. It was a vast playground in which boys could always find something new and different to keep from getting bored.

The vast majority of the valley, something like ninety eight percent, was owned in one way or another by the government and could never be built up in such a way to ruin the valley or make us feel crowded to the point of feeling pressured to move. And the quiet here was something tangible—no rush, no pressure, no stress. We had found our Eden, our place to come to the quiet.

In Wisconsin, too many friends, family, and church members had expectations of us that would have made the route we chose very difficult for everyone concerned. We decided that we couldn't stay there. The central problem was that our vision, our expectation, our dream for our life was very different from anything they had ever contemplated, and if you are going to embrace something different from society's idea of normal, you should plan on others misunderstanding you, even if they are doing so with the very best of intentions. Before you came to this stage in your life, you might well have held similar attitudes toward a friend or family member who joined some odd counterculture movement. So if you find yourself misunderstood, in the strength of Christ meet their misunderstandings with understanding and love.

Your Eden might not be a place in the mountains. You may hate the very idea of cold and snow, and if you do, then plan accordingly. Your place to come to the quiet might be a place near the beach on the Gulf of Mexico, or perhaps you love the flat Midwestern farmlands and a quiet home in Kansas is your ideal. There is nothing wrong with any of these places. What matters is having a place that is just right for you and who you are. The aim of relocation is to gain relief from the interference of others if that is a problem for you, to bring life down to the irreducible minimum and so redeem your time, and to find a way to give time to those things that matter most to you.

Sally and I chose the mountains, and perhaps it is a fitting symbol. The mountains have always represented escape from normal society and freedom from one's day-to-day responsibilities. Many of those throughout history who were drawn to the mountains have needed a place to run to, whether to escape persecution for their religious beliefs or to avoid prosecution for their illegal acts. The mountains offered a place of sanctuary. In our modern world however, all this has changed to a marked degree. While there are still two classes drawn to the mountains, they consist of those who seek their company on an ongoing basis because they meet a deep and usually very personal need of the human soul, and those who come to them occasionally to conquer the wilderness.

Those who come to the wilderness because they seek to meet the deeper needs of their inner being, myself included, engage in many of the same activities as those who come to conquer, and yet the philosophy of life could not be more different. Those conquerors see all the difficulties and struggles of this life as the price to be paid so that they may obtain their goal of standing upon the summit. There is no problem with their desire, but it does tend to rob one of the opportunities to enjoy difficulties while you are experiencing them.

Think about it for a moment. When we recount stories of our early years or even when those stories of our lives are not quite so faded, are not the stories that are most dear to us the ones that tell of overcoming incredible difficulties or seemingly insurmountable odds? And are not those people, those who stood by our side in difficulties—whose camaraderie with us was forged in the fires of affliction—the most precious to us? If this is the case, then perhaps it is logical to assume that such situations are, in and of themselves, rich and fertile ground for cultivating Christian character. I think so.

It seems simple, but the effect upon the life from these two philosophically differing views is easily seen in those who hold them. Most who have taken the name of Christ desire to stand at last upon the summit, but they do not seek out personal struggle or circumstances that will require self-denial or painful character development. Indeed, it is avoided as much as possible, and if unavoidable, it's trudged through in a manner that would make all companions wish that they were in a more tranquil environment.

Yet everywhere I go, people are drawn to my story and the idea of moving to the wilderness. Christian or non-Christian, American or foreign, the reaction is still a wishful longing of barely acknowledged desires, and the thoughtful person is bound to ask, "Why?" Why after all these many generations of city living does nature still exert so powerful a pull upon us?

Anyone who has ever raised a wild animal could answer our question easily: In every created life there is something that responds to one degree or another to the call of the wild. It is this type of life in contrast with nature that we were designed by the Creator's hand to live. God planted a garden eastward in Eden, and there He put the man and the woman He had made. This is our birthright, an innate part of what makes up the very essence of the human creature. If we are to find true satisfaction and happiness, it is more likely that we will find it in an environment similar to that in which our first parents were placed by God Himself.

I am not a dreamer living under the idea that everyone is going to be able to go live on a mountaintop with God and let the world go by. I fully understand modern society with both its benefits and its detriments. It is in light of the real-world demands on us and our families that I write this book, and in so doing, I am sharing my considered opinion that there is not one family in a hundred that is benefited spiritually, emotionally, or physically by living in the city. This does not mean that city dwellers are inherently evil, only that they live in a location that is far less favorable to the development of godly characters. In a highly urban area, it is nearly impossible to avoid the constant temptation of impure images, inappropriate music, and the insidious noise pollution that makes it almost impossible to hear the still, soft voice of God to the soul.

The reason I focus, for the moment, upon this topic is that it is the possession of the Godlike character that marks one as truly belonging to God. Character always comes first, and if we are to respond to the call of the wild in a manner that will bring us any lasting benefit, we too must place character development above every other consideration. This does not mean that we are to be perfect in the way we human beings tend to think of it. We must remember that the moment we come to God and surrender our wishes, surrender our plans and our wisdom to His, desiring pardon from our sins, then His great heart of mercy not only forgives our sins but covers us with the robe of Christ's righteousness, so that all that is seen is the beauty of Jesus and His life. It is God's design that we should grow up into the fullness of the Christian life within this covering as the faults and defects of our lives are dealt with in His timing. Because of this, we are considered perfect and holy, as the sins that remain are faithfully removed. As long as we consent to remain yielded and cooperating with His direction, surrendering up each new thing He asks for, we are His people and holy in the eye of heaven. Hence, when we consider the "call of the wild" we need to remember that it is a call to character development, to surrender to God, to holiness, not a call to some new reform known as "country living." The call of the wild is simply another of God's methods or tools to reach the human heart and draw it to Him that it may be transformed.

Hence there is an inescapable change that comes over one who chooses to live in the wilderness. I have seen it in all, whether openly religious or not. When people move or go to the wilderness for a while, they find the senses that are so dulled by city life start coming alive once more—especially the sense of hearing. When the mind is bombarded with the constant background noise that makes up modern life, the mind trains itself to tune out those things. Once the noise ends, hearing suddenly returns. Things you never noticed before suddenly take on significance. The gurgling music of the stream or the rustle of the leaves is suddenly loud, and in like fashion the voice of God is much easier to hear.

With hearing come new challenges that you may have never faced before. If you are used to tuning out His direction, it caused you no great distress to ignore it, but when His voice is understood clearly and His direction crosses your will, you will find you are fighting the greatest battle ever fought. The task of character transformation, which was what God called you out to achieve, has now begun. I have watched many a fine family move out, only to find this work so painful that they threw all of their energies into some other seemingly more pressing task, such as building a house or new outdoor pursuits. So many focus upon country living and make the fact that they live in the country their salvation, and in so doing, they lie not only to others, but even more harmful, they lie to themselves, for they come to believe that they have entered into the pathway of life while their hearts remain as aloof from God as if they had never come to the wilderness.

People who make it successfully in the country learn sooner or later that work can be a joy, and the sooner this lesson is learned, the sooner happiness will reign in one's life. Life in the wilderness is nothing, if it is not work. Almost every task outside of character development is harder to do in the wilderness than it would be in more civilized locations. If you want to garden in the city, you need only the ground. In the suburban areas, you might need a fence to keep out rabbits or maybe a deer or two. In the country, your fence must exclude herds of deer, raccoons, skunks, and a host of other creatures. And in the wilderness, we had all those and the elk and moose, plus bears.

One bear took a very strong liking to Sally's carrots and would politely leave large piles of tops for us when he had stopped by to dine. Discouraging a bear is not easy. The wildlife manager came out with a shotgun and beanbags, and together we climbed atop our greenhouse to await our uninvited dinner guest. The ranger waited until the bear had climbed over the fence and was just settling in to enjoy his meal, then he let loose with the shotgun-blasted beanbag.

The bear about jumped out of his skin. Talk about great reactions! Not bothering to climb the fence, he simply hit it like a battering ram, collapsing a whole section, and ran off into the woods. I sat there studying the fence and realized that the cure had been just as damaging as the problem, and at least as expensive! This is the way things go in the wilderness. Nothing is ever as simple or as easy as you would like it to be. I looked again at the ruined fence, and just then the bear stepped out of the shadows and headed back into the garden for more carrots!

Wilderness living allows one to find the humor in every situation and to laugh at problems and mostly at self. You find that all the troublesome things in the modern world have fallen away. We worry about our jobs, bills, health, children and their education, about their associates and influences. But God says, "Take no thought for your life, what ye shall eat, or what ye shall drink; nor yet for your body, what ye shall put on. Is not the life more than meat, and the body than raiment? Behold the fowls of the air: for they sow not, neither do they reap, nor gather into barns; yet your heavenly Father feedeth them. Are ye not much better than they? Which of you by taking thought can add one cubit unto his stature? And why take ye thought for raiment? Consider the lilies of the field, how they grow; they toil not, neither do they spin: And yet I say unto you, That even Solomon in all his glory was not arrayed like one of these. Wherefore, if God so clothe the grass of the field, which to day is, and to morrow is cast into the oven, shall he not much more clothe you?" (Matthew 6:25-30).

This is the central issue in coming to the quiet, wherever we happen to reside. Will we stop trying to run our own show and to control our own lives? Will we cease to trust even our own wisdom? Becoming distrustful of our own wisdom is one of the first practical steps in beginning the Christian walk, for once we finally find that our own ideas and our own reasoning are not trustworthy, then we are in the place where God can begin to help and instruct us in a new and more complete manner than we ever have experienced before.

When I came to the mountains, I thought I trusted God. After all, why else would I have followed His leading to come to the quiet? I soon learned, however, that I was very trusting in my own way and my own wisdom, and the Lord in His mercy enrolled me in the wilderness school of hard knocks, so I could learn the lessons He desired to teach me. If you and I could hear God describe us, we might well hear the words, "O ye of little faith." I didn't understand why I faced hardships, and it wasn't until later that I knew these things came for my benefit. Until then, all I could do was trust that somehow we were still on the right track. Privately, I thought about it all and wondered, *Why, Lord, why?*

CHAPTER 4

WHY ME, LORD?

As if a man did flee from a lion, and a bear met him; or went into a house, and leaned his hand on the wall, and a serpent bit him (Amos 5:19).

When Sally and I decided to move to the North Fork, it was not the secluded wilderness playground of the rich and famous that it is in danger of becoming today in similar fashion to Vail, Colorado, or Jackson Hole, Wyoming. Indeed, when we were searching for a place, only one private parcel was available, and it sold before I could even make an offer for it. I was discouraged because we had found our valley, the place we wanted to live more than any other, and there was nothing available. I prayed, but no miraculous solution appeared. Instead I just felt the impression to drive up the valley and that somehow God would lead. As I bumped and jolted my way over the terrible North Fork Road to the upper end of the valley, I surprised myself by obeying an impulse to turn into a dirt driveway that, like scores of other forest roads, seemed to lead off into the woods and end up nowhere. This road, however, ended at a little log home, which sat alone amid a small field of weeds. And there, mowing those weeds was a barrel-chested, powerfully built man, who looked like he belonged to the wilderness, yet was clearly well on in years.

Well, I thought, *I don't have anything to lose. I'll tell him what I'm looking for and see if he knows of anything.* He listened quietly as I rattled off my list—acreage, year-round water, a gravity spring, and, if possible, property that bordered government land, so it would never get built up nearby. After I finished, he calmly pronounced, "I'll sell you my place."

"What?" I stuttered, and he began to show me *his* place, which turned out to be nothing more than a tiny, roughly finished log cabin on five acres. *It's not as many acres as we want, and the cabin is small,* I thought to myself. *But then, this is an experiment for us. We should be able to survive, at least a few years, in this home,* I figured as he continued the tour. He showed me the creek and invited me to drink from it, handing me a glass. Even I knew that you never drink from an unproven source, and I was hesitant, so he grabbed the glass and drank it down in front of me. Then he showed me the cistern in the creek bed that supplied the house with water. I don't know if his intention was to impress me, but he was succeeding. I asked about a spring, and we walked up to a hundred-gallon-per-minute spring just high enough that it could provide gravity-flow water. "I've never done anything with it," he commented, "but anyone could rig it up." The property *did* adjoin Forest Service property, and it *did* have panoramic views of the mountains in both Canada and Glacier National Park.

The man sold me on the property even though it was only five acres, and even though he wouldn't come down in his price as much as I thought he should—and I'm a good negotiator. The cabin was probably the worst deal I ever bought. Yet I found myself signing the contract because you can't put a price on your dreams.

By the time my family was able to settle into the cabin and begin our new life in Montana, it was October, which in this high country is the beginning of winter. We did not have a sufficient wood supply to heat our house the whole season. All that first winter found me out in the snow trying to get more wood in. I wish you could have seen me. I'd carefully pick out and cut a tree.

With a snap and a crack the final fibers holding it upright would break, and the old giant would simply disappear. I remember just staring in awe as the entire trunk vanished in more than three feet of snow. I had to literally dig the tree out before I could even get the saw low enough to cut the trunk into sections. Then I had to somehow pry the chunks of trunk out of the hollow formed when the tree fell and roll them to my toboggan and then get them strapped down so I could tow the load home with the snowmobile. I could get about three big sections in each load, but that doesn't begin to describe the problems involved.

As I rolled each heavy section toward the toboggan, they accumulated so much snow it looked like I was trying to build a snowman rather than a wood pile. Snow got packed on the sections, and they gained so much weight that I could hardly roll them. Reaching the toboggan at last, I had to scrape it all off before loading each one. Despite the work involved, I grinned as I headed home with my first load.

Unfortunately my moment of triumph didn't last long because it was then I discovered that my wood lot was located uphill from my house and I had to tow these loads down a steep incline. *Bam!* The heavy load slammed into the rear of my snowmobile, pushing me sideways like some bizarre demolition derby. The impact caused the load to lose momentum, and it backed off slightly. I stole glances over my shoulder only to see it gaining on me once more. I had only covered a few more yards and *wham!* I was slammed to the left so hard I almost lost control of the snowmobile. What a lesson in practical applied physics I received as the force of the snowmobile and the load worked against one another.

My path home became a series of "S" turns as the rear fishtailed one way or the other at every impact. After a few loads, the pattern was so well set and the packed surface so deeply grooved into the three feet of snow that it resembled bumper cars on a bobsled run—and it got faster every run! There was one payoff though. It made a splendid sledding run for the kids, even if they could only use the bottom half—it was just too fast to start from the top!

One of our nearest neighbors was a family named Bernhardt. Mr. Bernhardt had lived many years in the mountains, doing whatever he needed to survive. His three sons were now young men, and together they had formed a contracting company that built many of the beautiful homes in this valley. I was fresh from the city, and I had to ask someone all my questions. So if I didn't understand my water system, I asked the Bernhardts. If a certain repair required an unusual tool, I was off to the Bernhardts'. I hate to admit it now, but the Bernhardts thought I was by turns the most useless, the dumbest, and the most naïve man who had moved to the North Fork in many a year. They always helped me, but there is a fierce independence among the residents of this valley, and in keeping with their philosophy, they helped only to the extent that they would provide me the tools and knowledge to let me help myself.

When I was cutting down trees that winter, I wasn't as skilled as I have learned to be, and I got the blade of my one and only chainsaw pinched good and tight in the heart of an old dead giant. By this time I hated to go ask the Bernhardts for help because they kidded and teased me so badly about being a stupid city slicker that I always felt like I walked out of there about six inches shorter than when I went in. Let me tell you, it was really a hard thing to have my pride hurt that way. So I tried to get the blade free with my wedges, but it was such a huge tree that a wedge couldn't begin to move that trunk, and at last, after much futile effort, I realized the time had come for another visit to the Bernhardts'.

As I trudged down toward their house in the snow, I couldn't help thinking of my prior visits and what this one would hold for me. Winter in the North Fork is a time for residents to sit around the table next to a stove, telling stories and sharing gossip while waiting out the long harsh winter. I didn't like to admit it, but I knew that a lot of the gossip this winter had been about my family. It seemed that everyone was taking odds about our chances of surviving out here, and most didn't think we'd last more than a year.

"Come on in, Jim," a voice called out from the house's interior before I could even reach my hand out to knock. I entered to see all four guys hanging out at the kitchen table, a crackling stove behind them. I exchanged greetings, and they all snickered when Bob asked, "So, what went wrong this time?"

"Well," I said trying to sound casual, "ever gotten your chainsaw blade pinched?"

Laughter erupted as if from a volcano. "Ever heard of wedges, city-boy?" came the first comment amid squeals of laughter.

I smiled and tried to laugh along, but my humor was only skin deep. "Yes, I heard about wedges somewhere along the line and even tried using them to get the blade free, but this tree is just too large. What I'd like to do is borrow a chainsaw to get mine free."

Bob willingly lent me his chainsaw, but Walter had the last word as I was walking away. "He'll be back in an hour or so when yours is stuck in that tree too."

I walked back to the tree knowing that this story was going to be passed around the valley, getting larger and larger so that by the time the last person heard it I would have a half dozen saws stuck in that old tree with wedges sticking out of every crack. The truth is that my saw came free in a few minutes, but that would never make the list of local gossip.

When we sold our home in Wisconsin to move to the wilderness, it took almost every cent we had to buy the land and transplant ourselves to it. We had moved to the wilderness, but there had been a cost to our downsizing because we had only six thousand dollars a year to live on for three years. This was all we had to begin our wilderness experiment, and from the start it was an experiment fraught with problems and trials much more common and much worse than any I had ever faced before. We had our very basic cabin and a secondhand truck. From the start there were unforeseen problems. The truck broke down, the propane tank sprang a leak, and we lost all our gas right after we had the tank filled. That winter was harsh, and the creek we got our water from started to freeze up. This forced another trip to the Bernhardts', who gave me bales of hay to insulate the creek, but it kept freezing up anyway. That began an epic and losing battle against the ice. I would go down and chip it out, and soon I would have to do it all over again. Eventually I had to get up every hour all night long and walk down the steep snow-covered hill in the dark (and I was still scared of the dark) to chip away at the tiny channel in the creek, trying to coax water into our cistern, but at last it was no use, and now I had to go at least once daily to pick up water from the Bernhardts'.

When I finally had our water restored, I entered into a major improvement for our home—a hot-water system. Now I had never done any plumbing before, but I had seen diagrams of how such systems worked in books, so I got the right type of copper pipes and went to work. The principle behind these projects is simplicity in and of itself. A convection system works by having a hot-water tank that feeds water from the bottom into your cook stove, and as it is heated it rises. The hot water is returned via piping to the top of the tank and, presto, you have hot water. In practical terms, the system is rather more complex, requiring just the right type of vent to properly heat the water and prevent a vacuum air lock.

I worked my design and, by late evening, had it assembled. I was excited and turned on the water expectantly. Can you imagine how I felt? The sense of accomplishment, the pride of inventiveness and self-reliance filled my heart! Well, the effect was rather like one of those fountains you see in city squares. Water sprayed in every direction. I had soldered thirteen joints, and twelve of them leaked! Now I have *always* struggled with my temper when things go wrong, and this was a trial that would tempt the patience of the *most* self-controlled man. "Turn if off! Turn it off!" I yelled to Sally as if it were her fault. Then I studied the leaking joints and the puddles of water on the floor. Even though it was late evening by this point, Sally said, "Why don't you go talk to the Bernhardts, dear?"

A few minutes later found me in their inviting home, explaining my problem amid whoops of laughter. "Come on, guys," I told them, "tell me what I did wrong. What was my mistake?"

"Moving to the North Fork, that was your mistake!" Walt shouted, laughing so hard that tears ran down his cheeks. When they had quieted, Bob said, "Tell us what you did."

So I began. "I fitted and cut the pipes." They nodded. "Then I cleaned and sanded them." More nodding. "Then I heated the joints with the torch and soldered them."

"You used flux before the solder, right, Jim?" asked Bob's wife.

"Flux, what's flux?" I asked helplessly, sending them all into a new fit of mirth. When they could talk again, they explained how flux draws the solder up into the joint, told me how I was to use it, and then supplied me with some to get started. By now, it was after 10:00 P.M., and Sally suggested that we just go to bed. But my not being bright enough to have installed valves to isolate the hot-water system meant that until this problem was solved we would have no water for anything. So I was bound and determined to fix this problem tonight or die trying, and given my past experience, it might well be the latter.

It took two hours for me to disassemble, reclean, and resolder the joints, and at 12:30 A.M., we turned the water back on. This time there were only two leaks.

For just two little leaks, I saw no reason to take the time to drain the whole system, so I got the torch and started heating the joints. For some reason I couldn't get them hot enough for the solder to flow. It was baffling, for I knew the right technique now and had experienced some success. *Maybe I just need more heat,* I thought, so I got another torch and had Sally hold it on one side, while I held my torch on another, but it still wouldn't work, and I was getting angry. *It is all Sally's fault,* I thought. *She just doesn't hold her torch in the right place or the right way.* At 2:00 A.M. I gave up and went to bed.

The next morning I walked down to Bernhardts' about breakfast time, my tail between my legs, totally defeated. I told them my story and they roared with laughter. "You didn't drain the system, did ya, Jim?"

"No, why should I?"

More uncontrolled laughter and even a few sympathetic smiles as if they felt sorry for anyone that dumb. At last, they explained that the water in the pipes carried away the heat from the torches as fast as I could add it. I walked back up to the house thinking about what God had been trying to teach me, and one lesson was clear. God was allowing these circumstances to humble me and make me teachable and perhaps, if for no other reason than that, my experience served a useful purpose.

Another home project I had to do was putting electrical wiring in the little room in our cabin that served as both storage and pantry. I read about the project in how-to books, but one question eluded me and that was how to know for sure which wires were hot and which were not. So I decided to ask the Bernhardts. "Here's what you do, Jim," Walt explained. "Ya lick your fingers and grab hold of the wire, and if ya feel a little current, ya know it's hot!"

This wasn't very satisfying, but these guys were contractors, so they must know what they are talking about. So I started on the job, and every time I grabbed a wire, my family heard me exclaim, "Ouch! Ooch! Ouch!" And all the while I did the job I kept thinking about how tough those electricians must be to do this every day! It wasn't until afterward, when I shared my thoughts about electricians with the Bernhardts and was greeted with hysterical laughter that I knew I'd been had.

I wish this had been the end of my problems, but it wasn't. Because we didn't want to spend any of our limited funds on such things as car repairs unless absolutely necessary, we drove around on such worn tires that all four went flat at once on the wilderness gravel of the pothole-filled North Fork Road. It must be a record for the most flats at one time. No one else has matched it, that I know of!

That old Dodge truck seemed destined to teach us many lessons. I was traveling away from home once in the winter, and Sally experienced a fresh snowfall. She wanted to plow out the driveway, but the truck just wouldn't move in any gear. She tried to put chains on the tires but didn't know how. She looked at the truck, and one tire seemed to be off the ground slowly turning while the others just sat there. She got out the snow blower, and it quit working the minute she tried to use it.

Finally she sought help from the neighbors, but no one seemed to be home. There were no phones in the valley. There are still no conventional lines, and this was before cell phones or even radio phones were common, so communication in the valley was by CB radio. Sally got on the CB and called down to a friend some distance away who said he couldn't come for days. This was hard on Sally, who is task oriented and wanted to get the job done. But

God had something better in mind for her than doing my work while I was gone.

God spoke to her in the quietness of her thoughts and explained that He wanted her to focus on the children and forget the snow falling on the driveway. Sally, right then and there, stopped worrying about the driveway and threw herself into making the home a happy place for the boys. Later that night, she heard from the man who said he couldn't come up until much later, saying he was on his way. He plowed the drive and then looked at her truck. All four tires were on the ground. He got in to try and put it in gear, and it worked just fine. He left that night thinking Sally was just nuts to think there was something wrong. But there *had* been something wrong, right up until she allowed God to redirect her thoughts and energies! Then the truck worked again. Little matter that others didn't understand the struggle she was having. Both of us were learning that sometimes we are made fools so that we can gain the heavenly kingdom.

I hated these problems because they forced me to face myself in a way I had never done before. Sally loved the life we were leading not because it was easy, but because she had the one thing she really had wanted and that was to have me home with her. The boys cared little except that they had both parents' attention for the first time in their life, and they loved it. I can't say I really loved it. Life in the wilderness was just a lot of plain hard work, and while I enjoyed the physical activity, the knowledge that we were living on very limited funds was never far from my thoughts.

To save money, we ate simply. We chose less expensive foods and always made everything from scratch. We didn't miss fancier foods and had enough to eat, so it never occurred to us how others might perceive our actions until the county sent up a large supply of food. They had heard about this poor starving family up on the North Fork. I absolutely refused it. After all, I had made a six-figure income the year before. I tried to explain to them that we ate this way out of choice and that intentional poverty so one could gain something they desired was very different from unintended, undesired poverty.

Then there were home repairs. One time we had a terrible smell and discovered the sewer vent pipe had become disconnected in between the kitchen and bathroom walls. There was a small access area in the very back of the kitchen cabinet that allowed the bathroom plumbing to be exposed, but it was not designed for the sewer vent. I got all the way inside this cupboard, trying, in a very uncomfortable, contorted position, to see the vent pipe and find where it was separated and exactly what I needed to do to repair it. To get an idea of what I was going through, kneel on a hard floor and crawl on your belly under the coffee table until it is centered over your back. Then stick your head into a bucket along with your arm that must carry the flashlight to see with and then turn your head between 90 and 180 degrees while coordinating this movement with the hand carrying the flashlight. I share this, not to excuse myself or to win your sympathy, but to help you understand the battle we face with our own self-will.

While I was down there, Sally, who knows even less about plumbing than I do, offered a steady stream of ideas that made perfect sense to her. To me, under the sink in the cupboard, they were the most useless things I have ever heard. Listening to Sally as best I could, I waited for her to be still a moment and then I shouted out of my deep dark hole, "Sally, not now!"

There were struggles of a more personal nature. Perhaps one of the hardest things for Sally was no longer being able to buy things like paper towels or facial tissue. Now in reality the few cents we saved by not purchasing these items would probably not have changed our economic status that drastically, and I see that now. But you must remember that just because we were seeking out the

Christian life didn't mean we had discovered it yet. I was still the same hard-headed German who had lived in the city, so my traditional way of dealing with a conflict was to state my pronouncement and then, like a dictator, demand no discussion about the decision I had made. Sally's method of dealing with these conflicts when I was not open to her point of view was to stuff down her feelings because she knew they could not find safe expression with me. For her, this lack of paper products seemed to be the ultimate deprivation, and she cried and cried when I told her we simply couldn't afford it.

The problem with stuffing down your feelings is that there is only so long one can do that before one's limit is reached. Every so often Sally's emotions would burst out in despair, offering me a window into the inner woman. I had no idea how to fix those problems! I was trying to look after the needs of the family as best I could, which was good, but at this point in my life I was very unfamiliar with looking after the more personal, emotional needs of my wife. One of the hardest things I had to face in the wilderness was my "self," and it took some months for me to see that Sally or my boys were not the main problem in our home—I was! I can't tell you how hard this revelation was on me. Call me to wrestle a grizzly, but don't ask me to face myself! That's painful!

Sally had to face a number of fears moving here. She was fearful of the bears, but also of much tinier creatures, such as mice. It so happened that we had a few mice in our wilderness cabin, and it would take some time to eliminate them completely. In the meantime, a mouse would occasionally pop out from under a kitchen cupboard and scurry frantically across the floor, eliciting a scream from Sally. "Ahhhh! A mouse! Jim!"

I'm logical, and I didn't want to stop what I was doing to come running to her aid. More to the point, I knew that the mouse would be gone by the time I got there, so I provided her with the solution. "Just step on it!"

Poor Sally! She wanted her white knight to rescue her, a fair damsel in distress, and what did she have? Me for a husband! She'd look at the mouse that was frantically looking for a hiding place, and as fast as it was, she knew it might require several stomps before she connected. Worse was the idea of feeling tiny little mouse bones crunching under her foot. Sally never did step on any, and we eventually trapped them all.

You see, we think that if we are on God's program we won't have any problems. The truth is that when one is truly seeking after God, the devil is aroused to fight against the loss of his subjects, and trials and troubles abound. We had come to the quiet but found ourselves lost in a storm of trials. Yet it brought us together as never before. It drove us to our knees. We found God's promises are true, that He will never leave us or forsake us. We found that adversity builds character and binds hearts together. Because there were no outside distractions, no employment, no TV, no phone—nothing but our family, nature, and God—we found a new freedom to love, to laugh, and to work, and for the first time in our lives became a *real* family.

In the past, I might have been able to take a few minutes with my boys, maybe to take them on my lap for a short time and let them drive the lawn tractor. Now I could have them ride with me when plowing snow, and they loved just being with their father. That first winter, we played like new friends. We built igloos and snow forts and had snowball fights. We sledded for hours and when it got too cold, we finally came in to dry out by the fire and play inside games. We read lots of stories and just enjoyed being able to have the time with each other. We were a real-life "wilderness family." We had left one life behind, and we were falling in love with each other and this new life.

Allow me to let you in on a secret. You don't need to give up your current life and move to the wilderness to gain much or even most of what we have found. It required us to make choices about our primary focus and what our goals and aims of life would be. These are choices that can be made anywhere. Were they easier to make in the wilderness? I think so, but some people have made those choices and refocused their energies without changing their location or employment. The key is to decide what your priorities are and then develop a plan to reach those goals.

Most of us look at what we are currently doing and then wonder how to force into that schedule the things we really desire—family time, time for our marriage, and true spiritual development. If we try to keep doing all the things we do now and just add new priorities, it will never work. It has never worked for anyone. Take a serious look at what you really want out of life. If you are like us, you will decide that things, money, and influence are not going to bring lasting happiness. Only peace with God and truly loving family relationships can bring true happiness. It is up to you in your specific situation to decide under the guidance of God's Holy Spirit what you will have to cut out to obtain them.

I and my family are not the pattern to follow. Only God should lead in your life. In sharing our story and how we followed God's leadership, no matter how unconventional, we hope to inspire others to seek God's will for their lives and how God wants them to *come to the quiet*. Millions desire to be closer to nature and to God. Just look at the nearly endless numbers of urban dwellers who come to camp in the national parks and other wilderness areas. They long to taste, if only for a few moments, the life we have embraced, which has so benefited our family. Some may feel the need to come to the wilderness; others may move to the country; still others may stay in an urban or suburban setting. Each of these choices brings with it some benefits and some problems. Country living will not solve your problems, nor is it your salvation. It is simply one of the many tools God uses to help us find Him. Not everyone is called to the wilderness, but all are called to find the same wilderness experience with God that we have found here in the mountains.

If you seek to come to the quiet and experience God in a new and personal way, know with certainty that whether you're in the wilderness or in the city, the devil will do all in his power to cause problems and difficulties, for he knows if you come to the quiet of God's presence and continue to seek a Savior for yourself and your family, then he will lose his hold on you. Don't be discouraged because things go wrong, for if the enemy of our souls is aroused to fight against us, then we can conclude we must be on the right track, and this is what makes him so very fearful. Seek God while He may yet be found. Allow Him to bind your family together in strong bonds of love and affection. Accept the assaults of the kingdom of darkness for what they are—an admission that you are indeed not far from the kingdom of God. Come to the quiet and find peace and rest for your soul.

CHAPTER 5

IN THY SHADOW

He that dwelleth in the secret place of the most High shall abide under the shadow of the Almighty (Psalm 91:1).

The grand secret to living the Christian life is learning how to live within the very shadow of Jesus. While it is easy to talk about in the abstract or as a concept, it is an experience rarely found and seldom sought, even by the most devout Christians. The experience, once glimpsed, will leave one with the desire for nothing else. So come with me and catch a glimpse of this special place—under the shadow of the Almighty. Perhaps there is no better place to begin than back before I had ever heard of a personal God.

"I just want to make one thing clear to you students. If there is one person who does not deserve a position in this field, it is Jim Hohnberger, and I will make sure he never works in this field because I will never write him a recommendation."

Even in the 1970s, when people spoke their minds more freely than in earlier years, such a comment by a college professor left the class dumbstruck. No one missed his message about being sure to stay on his good side. I didn't know this was going on until some friends informed me, and when they did, I got pretty hot under the collar. This was the lowest, most underhanded, unethical behavior I had ever heard of a college professor engaging in, and, worse, I didn't know what I had done that so raised his ire. It turned out that the Earth Day celebration was the problem. I had been thinking of transferring to another college because the Earth Day celebrations were not required there, so I took the free day designated for Earth Day and had gone to check out the other university. The professor heard I was gone, that I'd had the audacity to skip the Earth Day celebrations, and he was livid. Later I went to see him, and it was clear I had made an enemy. Granted, I only went to see him to defend myself against his slander. I felt I had done nothing wrong and that he was totally in the wrong. You can imagine how far we got with my attitude and his grudge.

At last, I decided to go see the head of the college and tell him my story. It was his turn to get upset—not at me, but at the unethical behavior of his staff member. He dealt with the man, and an uneasy truce resulted. However, I knew in my heart that I had handled it badly, and even though I had won, the entire episode left a bad taste in my mouth. I felt no elation at having gained the victory over the professor.

I didn't know any better way, even though I had gone to church for as long as I could remember. I didn't know that God wanted to be a personal presence with me and that He could help me through such situations. You and I are made up of our thoughts and our feelings. The issue each of us faces every day, in fact every minute of our day, is this: Who is going to rule over these thoughts and feelings? Am I going to use my human reasoning, or am I going to allow the mind of Christ to control my behavior and thoughts? Philippians 2:5 tells us, "Let this mind be in you, which was also in Christ Jesus." And 2 Corinthians says in chapter 10, verse 5, "Bringing into captivity every thought to the obedience of Christ." Therefore, it is clear that we are to do more than control our outward actions, and bring our thoughts under control also. The question I asked when this idea first became clear to me was, "How?"

I understood biblical truths and I knew a lot about God and the reforms of the Christian life. I had a strong will, and I could carry out many of them myself. But to control my thoughts, my feelings, and my emotions was impossible for me. Something would happen and I would get so upset that my reactions seemed almost automatic, and finding a way to break this cycle seemed impossible. But then I began to catch a vision of a totally different understanding of the Christian walk than I ever had before, and it transformed my life, not in the outward reforms, but in the inward life, in my thoughts and feelings. Here is how it worked.

God brought me to the quiet so that He could get me to "be still, and know that I am God" (Psalm 46:10). Here in the wilderness, it took weeks and months for us to unwind from the stresses of life, to calm down from the trauma of relocation, and to regain our physical health as we gradually adjusted to our new life. It was Sally who first started understanding just how God spoke to the human mind, and I was skeptical. After all, I was the man of the family, and God should speak to me if He was going to speak to anyone! When she started sharing with me the way in which God impressed her thoughts and did so very specifically, I decided I was going to go to God and get this experience myself.

I went up to my quiet spot in the house and I prayed. Then I concentrated on listening for God's voice, but I got nothing, and I mean absolutely nothing. I struggled to keep my mind from wandering as the minutes passed. When at last I failed to keep my mind open, I would pray once more and start the same struggle to keep my mind receptive. As I repeated this cycle an hour passed and I heard nothing. "Please Lord, speak to me," I prayed. Two hours and then three hours passed and I still got *nothing!* Four hours I stayed there on my knees. Four hours! And do you know what I received from God? *Absolutely nothing!*

At last, feeling totally humiliated and rejected by God, I gave up and went for a walk. OK, maybe it was more of a stomp than a walk at first, because I couldn't figure out why God would communicate with one person and not another. The one thing that had always drawn me to God was His fairness, and now I didn't feel like I was being treated fairly at all. Sally's prayers seemed to be a hotline to heaven, and mine seemed to get nothing but a recording stating, "Your prayer cannot be completed as dialed. Please check the prayer before repeating."

It was in this frustrated state of mind that I had the idea come into my head, *"Jim, I do want to talk to you."*

Now my own thoughts are mocking me, I thought, *How frustrating!* I got my mind back on the subject and muttered the prayer, "Why, Lord, why aren't You speaking to me the way You do to Sally?"

"Because you can't control Me that way."

These thoughts of mine are really messed up today, I fussed. *Where in the world did that crazy idea come from? Is it the Lord? No, it just can't be! God, is this You speaking to me?*

"Yes, Jim."

Well, why didn't You speak to me when I wanted You to? I spent four hours waiting. You didn't say a word!

"That's right, Jim. I didn't say a word so you would come to realize you can't control Me and I don't talk just because you want Me to. If you want Me to speak with you, then you have to consent to allow Me to talk when I know the time is right, not when you feel you should hear from Me."

This was how it all began for me. Sometimes in my past I knew God had spoken to me, but I had no idea how to have two-way communication before this experience. I came back home with my emotions exactly the opposite of what they had been when I left. I was on top of the world because God had spoken to me in the quiet recesses of my heart. While I didn't know or understand it at the time, I had taken a leap forward in learning how the human being lives under the shadow of the Almighty.

It was easier for me to hear that still, small voice when I wasn't rushed, when I lived in a quiet setting, but it was also essential that my mind had quiet. This is why Christianity has always done well in adversity and always stagnated under times of freedom and prosperity. When you are in a jail cell, when you are being tortured, your mind has nothing else to distract it from God, and this is why Western civilization has become one of the greatest hindrances to true Christianity. No place better symbolizes the values and benefits of Western culture than the United States, and here, in spite of religious freedom, in spite of material prosperity, in spite of literacy, in spite of denominational support, in spite of every advantage that should foster true Christianity, there is a famine in the land and a hunger and a thirst for true, vibrant, living Christianity that is a constant trust sustained by continual communion and appropriated by a living faith.

The United States of America may just well be the hardest place in the world to obtain the experience I am speaking of. Here there are so many things to distract us. It seems that every other billboard holds up before us the image of a gorgeous woman—usually in a state of undress. Magazines shout out to us from every retail checkout stand with the same type of pictures as well as the trash, trivia, and trouble of the rich and famous. All of these are designed to attract our attention. The female form is probably the most eye-catching thing in the world—woman, the crowning act of God's creation. And yet Satan has perverted the God-given beauty and attractiveness to the point where only the sensual is seen. Satan degrades men into little more than brutes. Even women's magazines are filled with pictures of beautiful women exploiting their sensual abilities and articles telling the female readership how they too can dress, act, and behave just like the models. Women lose their God-given reserve, which if preserved would shield them from a thousand perils.

Whatever we are, men or women, we respond to such things in an automatic manner. We have the same responses to the demands of appetite, to anger, to frustration, to touch, smell, taste, hearing, and sight. Our senses feed us information, and all our lives we have responded and acted upon their input and the emotions they stir within us, while it was God's intention that these senses would be conveyors of data, and the human mind, enlightened by God's Word and His Spirit, should then be acted upon by the human will and be the force that controls human actions.

I moved to the wilderness to find and follow God, but what I found myself doing in those first months was simply responding to events almost without a conscious thought. Sally would say something I didn't like, and I would respond almost like clockwork, and I wondered how I was ever going to break free from this cycle of failure.

I started taking much longer in my personal time with God. When I focused on the Person, I suddenly found I had much more to talk about with God than when I was just seeking out information. I had been a biblical scholar. Now I wanted to become a biblical saint at home, and that was a lot harder than simply gaining knowledge. Slowly I learned that God wanted me to surrender all my ideas and plans for my day, even my wishes and desires, to Him and let Him guide my life. I wanted to enter into the experience Isaiah referred to when he said, "The LORD shall guide you continually" (see Isaiah 58:11). This took me some significant time. I don't know about your flesh, but mine didn't want to cooperate one bit, and it often took me a lengthy period of time to become willing to surrender to such a change of heart. Yet, once I did, I had peace and contentment. However, if you think this was the end of my struggles, I have some news for you.

I became convinced as never before that we face a very personal devil, and he was determined to destroy even the tiny beginnings I had of this deeper walk. Over and over he created situations that derailed me even before I got to the breakfast table. I continued to fail until I began to realize that the benefits I received from surrender, and there were real and tangible benefits, were not sufficient to keep me throughout my day. I came to see that surrender was but the beginning step. I thought it was hard to give up my ideas and desires to God, but He wanted me to do more than just assent to His wisdom. He wanted me to cooperate in such a way that He could empower me to do more than mentally agree with Him. He wanted me to be able to walk in step with Him throughout my day.

My next step was learning how to take God with me from my worship, where He was very real, into my day. It took even more time to start finding success in keeping God a present and practical part of my day. Old habits easily reasserted themselves, and I found myself reacting without apparent thought just as I always had. Time and time again I strayed from His presence, and yet as I practiced keeping my focus on God and doing only His will, He started to become a very real part of my day and not just someone I stuffed away in the closet after worship. His voice throughout the day called for my heart again and again, just as the Bible said it would in Isaiah 30:21: "And thine ears shall hear a word behind thee, saying, This is the way, walk ye in it." If I yielded, I found victories where before there had only been bitter defeat. And so can you!

Repetition is good for learning, and you will have to repeat the unhappy process of drifting away and coming back to God throughout the day many times when you first start, because all your habit patterns and inclinations are bent toward doing things yourself and trusting your own reasoning and wisdom. I had to continually ask myself, "Is it going to be God or self running things today?"

Consistently allowing God to be present in a practical way throughout the day eventually results in our learning to make this a habitual experience, and with it comes the dawning of a new understanding of temptation. I used to think that temptation was all about a specific sin or action I was tempted to commit, but in this process I found that the specific sin is not really the issue. Satan's desire is for us to be separated from God, and he works to achieve this separation by keeping us active to our flesh and passive toward God. He doesn't care if this is achieved by us setting out with all our willpower to try and overcome the sin or if the sin simply rules over us with little effort. This is why there is so little true victory in the churches. The only way of success is to come to understand that every temptation is a call to separate us from God, and that is the battleground being contested.

God's desire is to take us from the condition in which our thoughts and feelings demand something and we jump to comply to a situation in which we ignore the demanding thought or emotion and agree to do only what God directs no matter how much it crosses our own will. Our willpower and determination are useless in overcoming the sins that threaten us unless we come to understand the area in which they have force. Most of us think our willpower is to be used in overcoming the sin, and that is where we fail. The only place that the will has power is in the freedom to choose. When we choose God's way, we are empowered through Him and by Him to do what we choose. Our wills can only pick which force, good or evil, will rule over us. With certainty one or the other always rules in every human life. It is the proper use of our will, our decision-making force, that frees us from the bondage of sin. If we can find this experience, all the forces of hell cannot overcome us.

The good news is that it is easier, much easier to find this experience in the quiet simply because there are fewer distractions. All of us can find our own place of quiet, even if it is just temporary, such as an unused corner of our house, or on a walk around the neighborhood, perhaps even in our own yard in the country, but we can find it almost anywhere we go because coming to the quiet is as much a state of mind as much as a location. Satan has been winning the battle of keeping us passive toward God, but once we understand his plans, we can turn the table and begin to be passive toward the ways in which Satan brings temptation, and that is through our thoughts and feelings.

So let's see how all this worked in the real world for Jim Hohnberger. When we moved to Montana, we did not plan on my immediate return to work. This was an experiment with God to see if we really could find Him. My first couple of years out were spent setting up our homestead and addressing myself to *my* character development and the personal reformation God wanted *me* to begin.

We lived very frugally for two years, and the experiment worked! However, funds were eventually going to run out. We might make it another year on what we had, but it was time to start looking for some type of employment. Through a number of divine interventions, I was led to start a real estate practice in our little valley.

Our valley runs about sixty miles north and south, and when we moved there was only about one year-round resident per mile. They were people who had been drawn to the area for many of the same reasons we had—the beauty, the clean water and air, as well as the isolation. There were some who viewed the whole valley as theirs, even though it was overwhelmingly government owned and hence it truly belonged to every citizen in the country. Many of them would have gladly put a gate at the southern end of the valley and would have given keys only to the fortunate few who already lived here. They had found paradise, and now they wanted to keep it to themselves.

My real estate practice was viewed by them as the greatest threat to their happiness, and they did whatever they could to stop me. Please understand, it was not all the residents who objected, just a few extremists. But they did make life very uncomfortable for me. Whenever I posted a sign on a listing, they tore it down. You must remember this is not your typical neighborhood where they were in danger of being seen by others and reported. The valley is huge, with very little population, so there were no neighborly eyes to question their actions, nothing to hold them back from trying to disrupt my business.

I decided to try and wait them out. I replaced the signs they took down, and they quickly removed the new ones. Before long, I had lost seventy-five signs, and there was a tendency to allow my mind to dwell on what these "terrible" people were doing to me. After all, they were taking down my signs, spreading all sorts of rumors about me that questioned my honesty and even my legality. They complained to the state licensing board about my supposedly illegal practice that I ran from my home. Even the state saw through this and told me, "It's just a bunch of jealous people. Ignore them, and they will soon go away." This might be true, but it was no easy matter to keep my mind from thinking about the evil things that were being done to me, especially when their actions were keeping me from gainful employment at a time when my funds were nearly exhausted.

I had found the valley of my dreams, and now that very valley was working against my efforts to earn a living for my family. When we face a temptation, we can focus upon the temptation or we can focus upon the solution. When we focus upon the problem, or temptation, it seems to grow larger and more difficult to control, just as rolling a little snowball downhill makes it grow larger and larger until it becomes so large, it gets out of our control. It is that way with every problem we face.

My choice was simple. I could spend my time trying to find out who these people were that wanted to, quite literally, take bread from my children's mouths; I could identify them and work to discredit them; and I could seek the sympathy of others and say, "Poor me" or have a pity party because I was being picked on. Or I could do the work God called me to do. I couldn't do both.

If I put the troubles out of my mind and surrendered them to

God and said, "Here it is, God. You handle it. It is just too big for me to take care of," then I could focus upon my real work. I can't control what other people do. I can't keep them from saying bad things about me. I can't keep a good reputation by defending it myself. I can, however, keep my mind focused upon God, and that is what I chose to do.

Every time a new rumor came back to me, every time I received a test, every time I had another sign torn down, I saw it as another opportunity for me to practice giving the situation to God. My mind wanted to dwell on the evil that had been done to me instead of yielding those upset emotions to God and staying at peace with my fellow men, even the ones who were tormenting me. I remembered the university professor I had been in conflict with. I didn't handle that situation well, and God was taking me over the same ground again and again until my choice to do things God's way was established as a habit.

I found out that you can *run* but you can't *hide* from the devil. Coming to the quiet and living in the wilderness or in a country setting will minimize the amount of contact and stresses you receive from other people, but it doesn't eliminate them. There is no place you can go to hide from every temptation. In this case, there was no way to avoid the temptation. Every time I bought groceries, every time I purchased gas, I knew I was that much closer to running out of money, and this raised all sorts of emotions in me, especially when I would find another sign torn down. I needed the money from the sale of these properties badly. Through hard experiences God was teaching me to be *passive* to the voice of my flesh—that is, to the voice of my emotions and feelings. At the same time, He wanted me to become very willing to listen and obey, to be *active* toward the voice of God speaking to me.

These trials never hit me when I was ready for them, such as during my worship time. They came when I least expected them to.

When I was driving along and saw another sign missing, my mind longed to mull it all over. I found that when I gave way and thought about it, when I told others about it, when I ran into friends and shared with them how mistreated I was or talked with my family back in the Midwest, the problems always seemed much worse than they really were. In fact, the longer I did this, the more disconnected from God I became. At last, I realized I was in a battle, not with my enemies, but for my spiritual life. I came to understand that God had not brought me to the wilderness so I could have rest there in my beautiful spot. No, God wanted Jim Hohnberger to come to the quiet of His presence so that I might have rest and peace in any circumstance, good or bad, and He desires the same for you.

Back in Bible times, David had fled to the wilderness, just as I had fled from civilization. David found he had enemies determined to destroy him even in the wilderness, and I also found I had enemies bent upon my destruction. The real issue for me was the same as it was all the way back in David's day: Can I find peace and rest for my soul in Jesus, apart from any change in my circumstances? Can I, by faith, entrust this whole ugly situation into His hand and not fret about it and simply trust God to take care of me?

I had just gotten to this point of understanding and the attacks got worse! More rumors and now even articles and editorials in the newspaper appeared. The things they said about me were so wrong and so biased that it was hard not to respond, and yet I had just promised to put it all in God's hands. This became my battle—not to fight the allegations, but to remain subdued and surrendered to God, allowing Him to lead and direct me.

The Lord brought my mind back to my grade-school days when we had fire drills. They seemed so senseless at the time, but people wiser than I knew we had to have a fire exit plan. Time after time, we practiced leaving the building in an orderly fashion and going to an assigned location, just so that it would be automatic if there ever was a fire. God made it clear I needed a "fire exit plan" for my thoughts, so that when this issue came up in my mind, I would respond automatically by taking my preplanned escape route. In my morning quiet time, God and I started planning what I would do when these problems arose. This way I *knew* what to do, and I didn't have to try and come up with a solution in the heat of battle.

I decided that every time I felt attacked, I would rehearse in my mind all the miracles God had performed to move my family to this beautiful valley, everything from selling our home at the price we needed, to finding the right purchaser for my business, not to mention leading us to the property and the little log cabin we lived in. I rehearsed these familiar stories from my past over and over until I was convinced that whatever problems I faced, I was where God wanted me to be and doing the work He had called me to do. This was the first phase of my escape plan.

I also used Scripture texts like Psalm 62:5, which says, "My soul, wait thou only upon God; for my expectation is from him." I would do more than simply recite the text. I would really try and enter into what the text was saying to me right then and there. That text says of my soul—my thoughts, my feelings, and my emotions, the sum total of what makes up Jim Hohnberger as a unique individual—wait *thou* upon God. Trust in Him, depend upon Him.

I discovered that God is interested in a very personal way in directing my day-to-day life. This willingness to direct and help the human being is referred to as grace. My part was to surrender to this direction and place my efforts by a freewill choice toward not only intellectually agreeing with God but cooperating with Him and abiding in Him, doing His will and not my own. This experience is impossible for us to enter into unless we choose it by faith. That choice then gives God both the legal and moral right to empower us to do what we desire in obeying His direction.

Finally I came to the place where I said, "Lord, I leave all my concerns over my reputation, the income I need, the unfair interference with my work, every concern I have . . . I will leave them all in Your hands, God, and I do so knowing You can take care of them for me."

"How long are you willing to do this, Jim?" the Lord asked.

"As long as it takes, I suppose."

"David spent fifteen years in this battle to prepare him for his life work, and, Jim, it may take a long time for your battle as well."

I didn't know it when I began, but the conflict was to rage for three bitter years. My signs continued to be torn down for three years. I became the most controversial and disliked person in the valley, at least in some circles, especially with the environmental extremists. During this time, I found there were times my escape plan was not as effective as I wanted it to be. It was usually a situation where a rumor would get back to me, so twisted and so distorted that it was ridiculous. I could mentally take my escape route, but the upset had aroused so much emotional energy that this alone disturbed my peace, or it did until I learned to combine my escape plan with physical exercise. While I cried out to God for deliverance, I ran or split wood. It was a huge help, and after vigorous exercise I found not only my mental outlook improved, but my mind was much more willing to cooperate with the program God had placed me on. My escape plan wasn't my salvation, but it was a powerful tool that continually reconnected me to God.

After three years, the conflict gradually started to die down, and it took me a while to figure out exactly how it happened. In time, I realized that as I had met my clients' needs and sold them property and they moved up to our area, they naturally viewed me as a friend who had helped them, and slowly, as the number of new residents increased, they outnumbered the vocal little minority that had been causing me trouble.

I found that while it may seem easier to "rest" in a wonderful location, say, in a hammock overlooking the Caribbean, with servants plucking perfect seedless grapes and dropping them into your mouth, this isn't true rest. You rest so easily there because of the stress-free situation and beautiful location. Eventually, I decided resting in the midst of ugly and unpleasant circumstances is even sweeter. Others can take away my hammock and my servants, but if I have found rest in Jesus, they can never take that away.

The disciples of Christ found this out one night. They were with Jesus crossing a lake when a terrible storm broke over them. The waves crashed and the lightning flashed. Amid the peals of thunder, they tried to sail the boat, but it seemed to have a mind of its own. They attempted to row, but the best efforts of these professional fishermen were useless. The boat began to sink, and only then did they turn helplessly to Jesus saying, "Lord, save us, we perish!" When they focused on their own efforts, the storm seemed even worse. When they focused on the real solution to their troubles, three little words from Jesus made the storm subside.

By doing the things I have spoken of, we starve the lower powers of our being. By lower powers, I mean our appetites, passions, and desires, which often rise up and demand we satisfy them. But there is more than just these because as situations create emotions and feelings, these too demand that we react to them. It is here that so many Christians find the upward life difficult. In nearly every case, the problem is that they feed these passions just enough to keep them alive. Starving them to death is your goal, and at first it may seem impossible because they are *so* demanding. I know it seemed that way to me when I first started surrendering my thoughts and feelings to God. I could hardly finish giving them up, and they were there trying to fight their way back into control. Depending on how upset I was, it could take hours to get them resolved with God, just surrendering them every time they came back up, over and over and over. Later, as I became more accustomed to doing it and the beginnings of habit were forming, it took far less. This battle is one you will fight no matter where you are. It is just easier in the quiet setting because there are fewer things to stir up your lower passions and conflicts that call forth an emotional reaction that must be dealt with.

Dealing with my work situation taught me how to gain the victory in every area of life, and it made me a free person. If you struggle with a quick temper like I did, your fire escape might be taking a walk or a prayer break in the bathroom until you are under the control of God. Perhaps you are troubled by lustful thoughts when you see a certain billboard displaying the female form, and your fire escape may be reminding yourself how wonderful your wife is. You might use Scripture to remind yourself that you were content with such things as you had before you saw that temptation. If you do these things, you will find, as I did, that you finally have found out how to have control over your thoughts and emotions. As you repeatedly overcome temptation, you develop the character of a spiritual conqueror, and you will find with new temptations that you are walking over familiar ground, where you know how to gain the victory.

This is why it is so important to slow our lives down wherever we happen to be, because at the pace most of us are traveling we just don't have the time, the energy, or even the inclination to enter into this type of warfare. Satan has intentionally designed life at this point in history to be so complex and so busy that it is nearly impossible for the average Christian, no matter how sincere, to take on the protracted battle of finding the secret place under the shadow of the Almighty. So they go to church and they desire to serve God, but in their thoughts, emotions, and feelings they are continually defeated. Hence, all they have left is an outward form of Christianity, and their lives deny the power of God to transform them on the inside.

If you are like I was and don't want your religion to be only an empty shell or a knowledge of truth, but an experience in Jesus that allows us to live in His shadow even amid the worst temptations, coming to the quiet is probably the only hope most of us have of finding what we really desire. Unless there is a total reformation of life's priorities, whether by relocation or reapplication where we currently are, it is a difficult thing to focus our energies in this new direction.

We must begin where we are. I would like to suggest that the best preparation to moving to a quieter location is to begin reordering and quieting your life right now. If you wait until you are in a better location, you may never start the slowing down process or simplifying your life.

Once you get started, you will face the battle of deciding every day and throughout each day who will rule in your life. In the past, it was Satan by default. Often we didn't even know how to end his reign over us, but now we have the choice. It is a choice you will have to reaffirm for the rest of your life.

Location alone does not make one righteous. The monks of old desired to cut off the temptations of the flesh by isolating themselves from the world. It didn't work because there is no righteousness in any location. Location has value only as it aids us in coming to and remaining in God. Will your present lifestyle allow you to gain this experience of full surrender and dependence upon God? Don't be too quick to say "Yes," because my next question is, has it done so already? If not, then you need to make plans to change things and get off the treadmill, freeing your time to really find God and experience the freedom that truly is in the greatest gift God can bestow upon a sinful being—living under the shadow of the Almighty.

CHAPTER 6

WE ARE FAMILY

And he shall turn the heart of the fathers to the children, and the heart of the children to their fathers (Malachi 4:6).

When we lived in Wisconsin, if anyone had told me that the people living in my home were not a family, I would have laughed in their face. Of course we were a family. We were just like every other family we knew, with the possible exception that we were financially better off than most because of our business. Back then the only ones I had to compare with were those about us, and they were all good sincere people with nice families.

The more fed up Sally and I became with the status quo, the more troubled we were about accepting the churches' and society's norm for behavior. Perhaps the thing that most troubled us was the way their children were turning out. Often they were slothful, unprepared for usefulness in this life, and even to human eyes, totally unfit for the heavenly kingdom. The parents were not in love with each other or their children. Some were divorcing, and others just looked defeated, dejected, and depressed. The children and parents seemed to be forming separate lives while remaining under the same roof. The more we watched others, the more we could see the danger signs of the same slow, insidious process happening in our home, our marriage, and our family.

By moving to the wilderness we hoped to regain that special something we once had. But how? After all the time that had passed;

after ignoring each other's needs; after leaving absolutely everything that used to make up our lives; after moving across the continent to a tiny home, how were we—four unique individuals with our own ideas, wishes, and desires, who didn't really know each other even though we thought we did, now that we were crammed into a small home in the long north-country winter, forced into close contact—how were we supposed to get along and form the family we had always assumed we were?

During the stress of relocation, I contracted double pneumonia, which laid me low for weeks. As I convalesced, I lay on one of the couches in the living room while the boys, just four and six years old, played about me. It was enjoyable in a different sort of way, a lot different from the life of work and committee meetings I had just left. I saw the boys during the day now, not just before and after work, and I was amazed at how bright and active they were. Suddenly one of them had climbed up on the back of the sofa and lay on the top for a moment before rolling off onto me with a laugh and a giggle. I tickled his little ribs, and he rolled off onto the floor, only to repeat the same process over and over, with his brother joining in. They'd never had so much fun, never knew I could be such a great playmate.

When I recovered from pneumonia, we started playing couch tag. We had two couches across from each other, and whoever was "it" stood in the middle while those on the couch tried to outwit them and make it across to the other sofa. You could have heard the squeals and peals of laughter from the peaks in the Rockies! This was how we started having family fun time in the evenings. At first it was just me and my boys playing while Mother looked on, but soon she joined in too. I started becoming a kid again. Freed from the former distractions of life, I felt free to enjoy my kids, to be a little silly and to throw off the mantle of seriousness and supposed dignity we adults seem to acquire, to reenter into the sweetness and innocence of childhood. The boys had a great time, and I found out that all they really wanted was *me!* The thing that is perhaps so shocking is that I had a great time too!

We started adding in a period of family worship at the end of our playtime. It was a simple fun time based on the age of our children. We would sing a song, pray, and read a Bible storybook. We would talk about the meaning of what we had read, and they might ask some childish questions about it. Then we would sing another song, and after another prayer, we'd tuck them in bed. As I said, it was a simple end to a fun-filled evening, and yet the impact upon our life was very profound. A bond was developing between us and our boys. When the spring melt came and the evenings were full of sunlight, we added outside games like kickball, tag, and bike riding to the fun activities we could do for family time.

One day the boys came to me with a great idea in their minds. "Father, Father, we want to chop down a tree."

"What were you planning to do that with?"

"We're going to use axes, of course."

I considered this for a moment and decided that with supervision, it would not be too dangerous. "OK," I said, "let's go find you guys a tree!"

Together we picked out a twenty-five-foot-tall, six-inch-diameter lodgepole pine that had clearly been dead for a while. I wish you could have seen them. You put a little hatchet in a boy's hands and he thinks he's Paul Bunyan! But they weren't Paul Bunyans, and they chopped and hacked at the tree for two days! At last the day of the big fall came, and shouts of "Timber" filled the air as the pine fell to its resting place. They were so excited and thrilled by their victory, they decided they wanted to build a log fort. So we selected more dead trees and laboriously chopped them down. These had to be cut to length, shaped, notched, and finally fitted. It took them all summer to build that first fort. We didn't need amusement parks, computer games, television, or videos to stay entertained and happy. Everything a boy could want was here. The same would have been true of girls. The activities may have been different for girls—they may have wanted to build a playhouse instead of a fort and take their dollies out to play, but the fullness of joy at having their parents' time and attention is not something limited to boys.

You know, I had viewed myself as a businessman, a socialite, an elder in the church, and certainly as an important man, but never as a father, a companion to my children. I hadn't even known about or aspired to such a position. But God in His own way had enlisted me in a training program, and I was learning, however slowly, to enjoy my own children.

I helped them build sandboxes, or maybe I should say they helped me build them. I was so out of touch that I thought they would just sit down and play automatically, but when the sandboxes were finished, the boys didn't know what to do. "I think you need to go out and show them how to play trucks, Jim," Sally said after a while.

"That's ridiculous! You want me to get out there and play in the sandbox?" She nodded. Feeling like I was about to make a fool of myself, I headed for the sandbox. Pretty soon we were all going, *"Vroom put, put, vroom, vroom,"* as they learned to make noises for the motors. I showed them how to use their miniature earth-moving equipment to make roads, towns, and cities. We constructed bridges and tunnels and played pretend. They loved it, and I was their hero, the person with the greatest ideas and the plans for getting the most fun out of play.

We loved being a family. We played hide-and-seek and kick the can. We read stories, not make-believe stories or cartoon characters, but the stories of great men and women of God. We sought out stories that would help build character in our children and that were entertaining for their age levels. As they grew, so did the complexity of the stories and the ability to start picking out the lessons for themselves. We played games like baseball and kickball, but in a noncompetitive way, and we added a whole host of outdoor activities like canoeing, caving, and tubing. We even built a raft to float on a beaver pond.

When they were still young, I started taking the boys on special father-son outings. We went camping, mountain climbing, and backpacking. I will never forget the first time I took the boys backpacking. We didn't have the right equipment, so I loaded their packs with big, heavy sleeping bags. They ended up carrying a lot of weight. But the weight wasn't as alarming as the size of the packs. The huge sleeping bags nearly dragged on the ground when hung on their little frames. Other people must have thought we were crazy, but the boys started out with packs that brushed their lower legs. I picked too long a hike for their first time, and they dragged along, complaining how tired they were, how far it was, and on and on and on. Of course, I was not the patient man I am now, who is seldom troubled by delay or annoyed by other's behavior toward me. Come on, I heard you. Don't laugh too hard at me! I have always had a weakness in my character to be impatient when things don't go as planned, and I soon learned through the boys' complaints that I was cultivating the same spirit in my children. They were just as impatient about enduring hardship as I was.

At long last, we arrived where we were to set up camp. I knew little about it in those days and had bought a little tent from a discount store for us to use. I didn't know that with tents, you get what you pay for. I didn't know about ground cloths to protect you from water underneath the tent. I didn't know how to pick a tent site carefully to avoid rocks under the tent floor. I didn't know anything about seam-sealing the tent. I didn't know any of those things that night as I lay down on the lumpy ground with Matthew and Andrew on either side of me and tried to sleep.

I don't know if any of you have ever gone fishing, but when you take a worm and puncture him with your hook, he squirms and wiggles like crazy, which is of course the thing that lures the fish to your hook. I felt as though I was fishing that night because several sharp, hook-shaped rocks were trying desperately to puncture my skin, and both boys were squirming and wiggling with excitement as if they'd already been hooked. I couldn't sleep with all this movement. Even when they settled down, the pain from the rocks just wouldn't go away. They seemed to have been diabolically placed so that no contortion of my body could free me from their grasp. I moved to get off one rock, only to find I had settled on another. At last I started to fall asleep in spite of the discomfort, and then I heard a noise no camper likes to hear. It was a *pitter, pitter, pat* sound that grew and grew until rain was pouring down. It fell as though we had been transported under a waterfall. My brand-new tent failed in the first few moments. It didn't just leak; it exalted in leaking and did so with such enthusiasm that I was sure the designer had planned it. I would have sworn at the time it actually funneled the rain in on us. I know how those poor people felt who failed to heed Noah's warning.

Through some curious ability—curious because it certainly could not keep water out—the tent did seem to possess an absolute talent for retaining the water it allowed in so freely. Before long the tent floor resembled a small swimming pool. Jolted awake and finding themselves sinking in this churning sea, both boys sought higher ground—me—and climbed on top, furthering the damage to delicate areas of my being that had already been abused by the rocks. I realized right then that whatever words I uttered would shape their idea of backpacking forever.

So I talked up the virtues of being real men and toughing it out in hard circumstances, of overcoming things like wind, rain, and cold, of putting up with being wet and uncomfortable. Thankfully they caught on to my words far better than I did, and we survived. We may have even managed to get a little more sleep that night. We returned home happy—cold, wet, and muddy—but still happy that we had conquered the worst the wilderness could throw at us.

That was our first father-and-son outing. I share it so you can see that even with the best of intentions, things do not always go smoothly, and it is our attitude in times of stress and difficulty that will determine how our children react to similar situations throughout their lives. I was becoming a father, a real father to my children, and I found it was even fun—if you lived through it, that is.

Being a family sometimes means helping children imitate adult roles and responsibilities. The boys loved to lay their heads in Sally's lap and have her rub their backs or run her fingers through their hair. This not only satisfied their need for human touch, but it was great fun to tease Father. They expected me to be jealous of my wife's attentions, and I didn't disappoint them. I would complain saying, "Come on, guys, she is my wife after all." They'd giggle and take delight in winning their mother's affection, which is not only the right of childhood, but training for their future roles as men in learning to be sensitive and enjoying the little affections.

I remember the day, when the boys were still quite small, they asked among several thousand other questions, where oil came from. I explained how it is obtained from deep wells.

"If you were looking to find oil, would you have to dig all the way to the other side in China?" they queried.

"No, just about half way," I responded casually.

"Father, might there be oil under the ground here?"

"I suppose it is possible."

"Let's go dig!" they shouted.

"Boys, you can't dig deep enough to find oil."

"Father, is every oil well real deep?"

"No, but it is still deeper than two boys can dig."

"We'll show you, Father. We'll find oil."

I couldn't help smiling at their enthusiasm. "If you find oil in our yard, I'll pay you a million bucks," I said with a laugh.

They rushed out to get tools and soon were "drilling" for oil in the driveway. Matthew got his well about twelve inches deep and began to get tired, yet he wanted his million bucks, so he decided to help the situation along. He went into the garage and found an oil can with a long flexible spout. Taking this, he partially filled his well with oil and then came in and announced he had struck oil. The oil he had added was utterly transparent, but I played along—for a while anyway. "Sure enough that looks like oil, but it is only seepage. You need to hit the vein and have a gusher." So Matthew had to keep digging. Andrew, being younger, decided he had to get his money as well, so he wanted to fill his hole with oil too. However, his brother had emptied the little oil can. Undaunted, he opened a new quart and filled his hole. When called to inspect his "well," I looked carefully at the hole and stuck my finger in the oil to examine it. I smelled the oil and announced, "Boys, this is refined oil. It doesn't come out of the ground this way." I walked into the garage and found my empty oil can.

"Do you boys have any idea why my oil can is empty?" Two pairs of eyes serenely disclaimed any knowledge of the event. "Now Matthew, now Andrew, we have always raised you to be honest and to tell the truth . . ." You can imagine the rest of our talk, but it was a wonderful chance to learn the value to telling the truth and not cheating even to obtain a great reward.

Kids learn best through experience, and if you have children, you can rest assured they are going to do things that seem odd to us as adults, and they seem to find danger in the most unlikely of spots. Boys just love adventure and danger, and they can find it in the most unusual locations. Children seem to attract disaster, even seek it out, and as a family you will survive or fail on the basis of how you handle it.

Our sons loved to play in the meadow just south of us and along-side the creek that runs through it. At one time beavers had dammed a section, and the area behind the dam had accumulated a large area of silt. Even though the beavers had moved on, the silt remained as a deep, inviting, wet, and murky mass of quicksandlike mud. Matthew and Andrew used to play in this area a lot, and like most boys engaged in such activities, perhaps it was best we didn't know about it back then. For example, they often set off in rubber boots to wade the creek, the object of the game being to see who could find a place to stand in which the water came closest to the top of the boot without overflowing. Both the winner and loser in this game ended up with wet feet. One day as they walked along the creek, they found the quicksand, and both of them started sinking. Matthew, being a little older and stronger, managed just barely to extricate himself, while Andrew could not. Matthew managed to get him out by laying logs on the mud and standing on them to pry him loose. Andrew's boots remained buried deep in the muck. The boys used sticks to dig them out, and after a rinse in the creek they were good as new.

Now that the danger was over, the boys decided this was a great place to play and dared each other to run across the water-logged silt, which was in places apparently deeper than they were tall. Many times one or the other had to be rescued by his brother and have his boots dug out. Even in this strange way, they were learning the joys of interdependence.

The boys rode bikes all year long, but what set springtime apart was the dirt and water thrown up by their tires. It got so bad that they would come home with a black stripe running from their neck to their rumps. Sally grew weary of trying to wash out the stains and threatened to have them wash it out themselves if they kept coming home looking like that. Matthew, who even back then was a great negotiator, reasoned that it wasn't fair that they couldn't get a little bit dirty. After all, we did have dirt roads, and Sally agreed that a little dirt was OK, but no more coming home looking like a black-striped skunk.

The boys didn't come home nearly as dirty after that, and we considered this a parenting success until many years later, when we found out what was really happening. They played the same as always, but before coming home, they looked around for a snow drift that hadn't yet melted and in the clean, abrasive snow, they would "scrub" their clothes until they were just "dirty" rather than "filthy," and then dressed in these now "clean" clothes, they would arrive at home in high spirits. It would take too much time and space to tell you about the boys parachuting off the greenhouse roof, digging an underground fort, and my being crowned king by my loving wife and admiring boys. The list goes on, and it's all a wonderful part of being a family!

When I worked one day a week in town, we often left the boys home while I worked and Sally shopped. They were getting a little older now, and the long drive coupled with the influences they were exposed to made leaving them at home with their chores and schoolwork a much more appealing option. If your family is constantly exposed to the worldly influences, you may not even notice it anymore. But we saw the boys pick up behaviors, mannerisms, and attitudes in just a few hours in town that often took days of prayerful work to undo. Together we decided that until they were a little more mature spiritually, we would spare them the influences of the town trip as much as possible.

Of course leaving them on their own carried inherent risks too. There was the day one winter when the boys found they had trouble keeping a fire going in the wood stove. It burned just fine with the door open, but no matter how well it was burning when they shut the door, it would slow down to where it was hardly burning at all. Concerned that they wouldn't be able to keep the house as warm as they should, they kept working with the fire and stoking it. Unknown to them, the damper on the stove pipe was virtually closed, and the fire couldn't draft properly. With nowhere to vent, the heat in the stove built up until the stove pipe was glowing red hot. If you visit our home, you can see the scorch marks on two or three of the logs in the wall, even though we repaired the damage as best as it is possible. A little knowledge proved a dangerous thing for the boys, and we realized they needed some more instruction in the care of the wood stove before they burnt the whole house down.

On another town day we had left them the job of weeding in the greenhouse. Matthew had stepped out of the greenhouse with a bucket of weeds headed for the compost pile when he saw a skunk trotting toward the back of the garage. It took refuge under our aluminum canoe, which was leaning up against the outside of the garage.

"Andrew, Andrew, come quick!"

"What is wrong?" Andrew asked, straightening his back from weeding.

"There's a skunk by the garage, and if you don't get it out of here, it is going to stink up the whole place. And it will be your fault!"

This was Matthew's favorite way of manipulating Andrew into doing his dirty work, and it worked for years. Together they checked out the situation and thought of all sorts of ideas, from throwing sticks and stones at the animal to heaving rotten produce from the compost bin so the smell of the rotting items would make the little creature decide to leave. None of these seemed very practical, and at last they decided that because a skunk looked rather like a cat perhaps it too would not like water.

Rushing about, they connected sections of garden hose until they had enough, and, after attaching a nozzle, they managed to manipulate the hose like a long flexible spear and shove the end of the nozzle under the canoe at this poor frightened creature that only wanted to hide. They turned the water on, and they were proved right. The skunk didn't like water. It fought back in the only way it knew against this strange snake that sprayed water. Unfortunately the snake didn't respond like any wild animal when sprayed; it kept right on antagonizing her. So this harmless little animal let loose on the offending snake an even larger dose of her "medicine."

Far from being discouraged by the unfortunate turn of events, the boys were driven into an even more desperate frenzy to get rid of the skunk. After all, it was now doing the very thing they feared and stinking up the place.

"Andrew, you go over and lift the canoe off her, and she will run away."

"Me? Why me?"

"Because if you don't get rid of her she is going to stink this place up even worse and it will be entirely your fault!"

"I'm not going to do it!"

Andrew may have been gullible, but at least here he showed good judgment in self-preservation. You can imagine what would have happened to this kid had he walked over and lifted the canoe.

"Hey, I have an idea," Matthew said, changing tactics to accomplish his goal. "I'll get a rope, and we will just pull the canoe off her."

He ran into the garage and came back with a brand-new hundred-foot nylon rope. "You go and tie it on."

"Why me?"

"Because I have to watch to make sure she doesn't get out."

"But isn't that what we want, Matthew, for her to get out?"

"Of course it is, and if you don't tie that rope to the canoe she is going to stink this place up even worse than she has already, and when Mother and Father come home, it is all going to be your fault!"

With trepidation, poor Andrew sneaked up to the backside of the canoe, tied the rope, and set a world record for covering the hundred feet of his escape route. The boys determined to play it safe. They stood at the very end of that hundred-foot rope and pulled for all they were worth, and nothing happened. The nylon rope just stretched. They took a couple of steps backward and pulled once more, and the rope simply stretched. At last, when they pulled on the rope the canoe toppled over, and the skunk defended itself against what it perceived as an unprovoked attack by the garage wall.

Scent glands nearly emptied, the skunk ran off, and the boys surveyed the damage. The garage wall had been hit hard, but it didn't compare to the canoe interior. It was literally painted a yellowish-orange color from all the spray. The very air seemed destroyed. It made the boys' eyes water even though they had somehow managed to avoid getting directly sprayed in the battle.

We usually called the boys around noon to check in and make sure they were OK. "How's everything going?" Sally asked.

"Could you pick up a case of air freshener while you're in town?" Matthew blurted.

"A case, Matthew? Why?"

"A skunk came by and stunk up the place."

"You boys didn't get sprayed, did you?"

"No," he answered truthfully, but certainly without full disclosure.

"Well then, I'm sure the smell will be gone long before we get back from town."

Meanwhile the boys tried to make sure that their mother's prediction would come true. They hosed down the canoe and the garage wall. They rinsed the whole area liberally, with no effect. Matthew remembered hearing that tomato juice removed skunk odor, so they applied that to the wall and canoe, but the air still reeked. How do you deodorize the air, they wondered. Then they began experimenting. I wish I could have seen them at work. They told us later about dancing around about the yard with tomato juice, tossing it in the air to purify it of the skunk smell.

Because of Sally's call, we had been warned that something had happened. Had we given more consideration to the specifics of the conversation and read between the lines better, we might just have stopped for that case of air freshener, but we remained blissfully unaware of exactly what had gone on until we pulled up to the house and skunk odor strong enough to curl your hair hit us immediately.

I told the boys their punishment was to clean up the canoe, but privately I had to laugh. If they had just left the poor little skunk alone, it would have gone away on its own. Skunks are generally polite, useful little creatures. Perhaps it takes an adventure like this to teach boys that some things are better left alone.

If you can stand another story of misadventure while Mom and Dad were away, I will tell you about Matthew and Andrew's fly-killing adventure. I don't know exactly why boys are fascinated with killing flies (not that I have any sympathy for flies, as they are filthy insects), but boys have been finding inventive ways to kill them for decades, if not centuries. Perhaps it is the thrill of hunting or maybe they feel gladiatorial, but whatever the reason on this particular day, the boys spotted a bunch of flies congregated at the window above the workbench in the garage. Instead of just swatting at them, they took a book of matches and decided to scorch them to death.

This worked OK, but on the bench where I cleaned paint brushes and mechanical parts, I kept a tin can with some gasoline in it. After a few attempts, the boys decided that they could boost the effectiveness of their matches by dunking them in the fuel before using them, and they were quite right. This is what they did until they ran out of matches in the little book they were using, and with the last match, they lit the paper book cover on fire. Matthew used this until it started to go out, and, wanting to refuel it before the flame was fully out, he dunked it in the can of gas.

Boom! The sound and the gush of flame and smoke drove them both off the bench where they had been sitting to roast flies. They looked back at the can, now sporting a three-foot flame like some berserk candle, black smoke pouring up. Matthew, with his hair and eyebrows scorched, tells his little brother, "Andrew, you have to get that out of here."

"Who? *Me?*"

"Yeah, you! If you don't get that can out of here, the whole garage may burn down and it will be your fault!"

Poor Andrew. It took years for him to catch on to the idea that his brother wasn't always being forthright about whose fault things were. He grabbed hold of the burning can and started to carry it out of the garage. Only because the can still held a lot of fuel was he able to grab a part that wasn't too hot, but it was still an incredibly dangerous thing to do. Holding it at arm's length, he carried it outside to the gravel driveway and managed to deposit the flaming torch on the ground without spilling it, although now he was as scorched as his brother.

"I know what to do," said Matthew as he ran for the hose like a firefighter. He poured water in the can, but it didn't go out, and then the flaming can of water and gas fell over and at once the entire gravel drive in front of the garage was a seething mass of flame. Both boys just stared at each other in astonishment.

"Guess that wasn't such a good idea," Matthew commented soberly.

Eventually the fuel burned up and the flame died out, leaving my two young men to study the results. There was a huge blackened area of gravel, so they got rakes and worked until it no longer showed. Next they entered the garage, and aside from some smoke, the building seemed remarkably unscathed. They looked at the can and, taking a wire brush, managed to remove the soot. Next they refilled the can with the same amount of fuel and returned it to its proper position on the work bench. Then they began repairing themselves. It took some effort with tweezers and scissors to make themselves look normal, but their efforts seemed to be well spent. When Sally and I came home, we didn't notice anything amiss.

It wasn't until the next morning that the boys came to me and somewhat sheepishly confessed to what had happened. I didn't punish them, other than charging them a few cents for the fuel they burned. In truth, I wanted to celebrate. They were still tender-hearted enough that they could not bear the unconfessed sin on their conscience. For that I was very glad.

Some of you are no doubt wondering why we allowed the boys to continue to stay home when these types of things happened. First of all, these were not weekly occurrences, but something that happened once a year or so. Second, and even more important, a sense of responsibility is very important in the formation of any family. Responsibility should be given to young people by their parents and should not be withdrawn the first time there is an error in judgment. Rare is the young person who, when given trust, will not try to live up to the trust, and so it proved with Matthew and Andrew. Yes, they made mistakes and did some very dangerous things; however, they learned to be responsible members of a family, and through their misadventures they gained great lessons and valuable experience.

Sally's interaction with the boys was just as involved as mine was, but in a lower key and more feminine manner. She played rough-and-tumble games and sports with her menfolk, but she also taught us how to do arts and crafts and even enjoy them. She loved to go skating with the boys and would often ice-skate on the frozen creek with them. As they grew older and more adventurous, Sally kept pace. She went scuba diving, dove off high-diving boards, really took part in every activity we did until we decided to go skydiving. At last she said, "No," and we didn't blame her. She did drive with us to the airfield, and on the way she changed her mind and decided to go with us. I wondered how she would do, but she didn't hesitate and stepped right out of the plane with her instructor. She had a parachute that could be controlled and steered to a degree. Sally loved turning this way and that in the air. After she landed, she was so sick from the motion that she was miserable for twenty-four hours. She paid a high price to be part of the family that day.

As Sally's story demonstrates, becoming a family means we don't always enjoy everything that the family does. Andrew fell in love with mountain biking, and even though I really do not like to ride a bike, I purchased a mountain bike so I could ride with him and be involved in things he likes. One year for our father-and-son outing, he decided we should go bike camping up at a lake on the Canadian border. "It will be no problem, Father," he reassured me. "We just follow an old logging road." What he didn't tell me was the old logging road hadn't been used for the better part of the century. It was filled with Kelly humps, which are piles of dirt placed to prevent motor vehicles from using the road. These made for an interesting ride, especially since bushes, shrubs, and even small trees had grown up during the years, frequently hiding these lumps and bumps until you rode over them. Sometimes the brush was taller than we were. It clung to our handlebars, trying to turn us and rip our packs from the bikes. Yet we pushed doggedly forward.

After what seemed a day of uphill struggle, we made it to the lake and set up camp. I was exhausted. My legs hurt, and my back longed for a chiropractor. I was even stiffer and more uncomfortable the next day when Andrew announced, "Father, let's really get going today and see just how much mileage we can do."

"What do you call what we did yesterday?"

"Oh, it was OK, but today we need to really push ourselves." I nodded weakly. I don't know how this is possible, but I am certain that the trip there was uphill and so was the trip home! I survived and enjoyed Andrew because we are family.

Then Matthew started reading Sam Campbell's books. He talks lovingly of the Canadian canoe wilderness north of Minnesota. In several of his books Sam tells of his search for a perfect lake at which to study all sorts of wildlife up in the wilderness. He always referred to it as Sanctuary Lake even before he found it. In one book Sam Campbell speaks of their expedition just after the close of World War II, when they discovered this special lake. The second trip to Sanctuary Lake is described in another book, which adds more information about the lake, its surrounding shores, and tantalizing hints of how to find it, with no real concrete information to go on, other than that it is somewhere east of sunset and somewhere west of dawn.

The romantic idea of finding Sam's Sanctuary Lake struck home with Matthew and became his dream, his goal, and it stayed with him for years. He started trying to locate the characters in the books and found that most of them had died. In the Quetico Provincial Park, as Sam's canoe wilderness is now called, everyone had a different idea of where it might be. Over the years, many people had claimed they had found the "right" lake, but none of the lakes had ever panned out. There was always something missing or something wrong with the description of the lake in question.

Matthew, after years of careful and sometimes not so careful study, had narrowed the possibilities down to just a few locations, and while I didn't support the idea of going to the Quetico at first, the Lord finally got through my stubborn spirit and made me realize that this was a way to be a family, to join in my child's dream, not grudgingly or half-heartedly, but with enthusiasm and excitement. I told Matthew that if he would plan it, we would set aside ten days to spend in the Quetico looking for Sanctuary Lake. Matthew was delighted!

There aren't a lot of clues in Sam's books, but after boiling it all down, he says the route leads off the shore of a famous lake along an animal trail to a small, very muddy pond. The pond ends in a small stream so choked by reeds that they had to force the canoe through it by prying with paddles along the bottom. Sam and his party dubbed this the River of Ten Thousand Umphs, after the noise made by the paddlers as they exerted maximal effort with each thrust just to inch the canoe along. Then, once through this weedy mess, you are supposed to cross six beaver dams and their ponds. After traversing the last pond you are to follow the stream again until you come to a small lake walled in by high granite cliffs. Somewhere there should be a name, "Joe," scrawled by an old Indian guide who gave the Campbells the secret of Sanctuary Lake.

Some days and many miles and portages later we found Matthew, our expedition guide, ready to lead us down the animal trail, except that it was not in use as it had been in the days of Sam Campbell. Fifty years had mostly obliterated the trail, and only some significant searching showed the way to the little pond, which is still very much as Mr. Campbell describes. We could see the River of Ten Thousand Umphs straight ahead, and everyone started to get excited, especially Matthew, who had worked so long and hard for this day.

Unfortunately, the river ended in a large field of swamp grass, reeds, and brushy trees, instead of beaver dams and ponds.

Matthew's disappointment was crushing, but he wasn't quite ready to give up. "We may as well walk from here," he commented. As he stepped out of the canoe, unknown to us, he was praying. I don't know his exact words, don't think he even remembers them, but it was something along the line of, *Why, Lord? I was so sure You had guided me to this spot. Why is there this meadow where there should be ponds?* The going was hard in the swampy field. The only mode of travel was hopping from grass clump to grass clump. After a hundred yards or so, even Matthew tired of the effort and stopped on some blackened branches, still hoping and praying that he might be on the right track, even though his eyes told him it was useless.

A noise in the grass made him look down. There was a frog struggling through the grass, hopping over the rotting sticks to plop in the water by Matthew's feet. Matthew's gaze went down, and he bent to look closer. The sticks had been cut by a beaver. Suddenly he was nothing short of a wild Indian!

"I'm standing on top of an old beaver dam!" he called back to me. He raced ahead, finding dam after dam. Fifty years had so altered the landscape that the ponds were completely overgrown. We found a moose path on which to portage our canoe, and at the upper end of the valley we found the stream again and floated into Sanctuary Lake. We found on this and other trips nearly everything Sam Campbell spoke of, even Indian Joe's name on the rock. It was faded and hard to read, with the O almost obliterated, but the J and the E were clearly there. Matthew had fulfilled his dream, and I found that for all my protests against going that I fell in love with this huge wilderness. We have returned nearly every year to vacation and relax amid its scenes of beauty and commune with the God who formed it.

When you enter into your children's dreams, you will bind their hearts to yours. Children always have a warm and ready reception when they know you have a serious, sincere interest, not just in your ideas of their happiness, but also in theirs. I have found that entering into their dreams and plans is by far one of the best ways to govern our youth, far better than dictating or nagging them. Our goal as parents is to take them from dependence on us as children and help them transfer to a dependence on God, the Mighty Counselor and their never-failing Source of strength as young adults. If we can give our youth this experience, we have achieved greatness in the eyes of the Lord both as parents and as families. You will have become a patriarch and will have raised a new generation of patriarchs. Your family will be one marked by heaven as serving the God of the universe, and you will be repaid many times over in happiness for any self-denial required.

However, a family is more than just a relationship with your children. It is a relationship of love between two adults. It was your good times together as husband and wife that made you parents, but too often love fades when the children come along and life gets busy.

Sally and I were determined to fall in love with each other once more. We started swing time, which I have talked about in my other books, as a special time to visit each day. We began writing notes and doing the special little things to draw out our affections. We resolved the issues we had between us and gave each room to be who we were before God. We left the past behind us to rebuild a better future.

We began to play with each other and not just with the children. A psychologist might refer to this as a re-emergence of juvenile play patterns, but we called it fun. We romped, we flirted, even chased each other, and gradually the distance between us disappeared and the hurt feelings faded. We had always loved each other, but now we were in love with each other. We started habits that continue to this day. We started swing time at noon and every morning and every evening we have snuggle time. We cuddle and enjoy one another, visit about our day and just enjoy being close. In our old life back in Wisconsin we didn't always want to be close, especially when we were harboring upset feelings. Now peace and harmony existed between us in a way that we had never experienced before we made becoming a real family our priority. It's a lot different from when we assumed we were in love and were a united family just because we shared a bed and raised children together.

My boys are married now and have their own homes, not much more than ten minutes apart from each other, although they are a little more than an hour from us. Not that long ago Sally and I spent the weekend with them in Matthew's home. We'd had a lot of fun, but on Sunday afternoon I was ready to head for home. Both boys tried to talk me into staying longer, just wanting to enjoy us a little more, but I saw no reason to delay and prepared to leave. Matthew hopped up and said, "Well, at least wait a minute. I've got something out in the garage I want to get for you." He was back in a minute, his hand behind his back. He looked at Andrew and nodded. Out came Matthew's hand holding a coil of rope, and both boys jumped on me. They tied me up and said, "There, now we have you to ourselves a little longer." My boys are men, but they still enjoy their family time that much. They didn't want us to leave, even after a whole weekend of being together. That bond was developed in those early years, and today it's unbreakable. They love me, and I love them. There is nothing they wouldn't do for me because there is nothing that I haven't done for them. That is what it means to be a real family. I hope it describes yours. If not, make it happen. In God's strength you can. May His most bountiful blessings attend your efforts, and may you say with us, "We are family!"

CHAPTER 7

A SIMPLE LIFE

Because they have no changes, therefore they fear not God
(Psalm 55:19).

Before moving to the mountains, we lived on forty beautiful acres in Wisconsin, and behind our large log home we had a bird feeder at the edge of the woods. Like most bird feeders, it seemed to appeal to the squirrels as much as the birds, and they visited it several times a day. I enjoyed watching them almost as much as I did watching the birds, and I noticed that each squirrel had his own personality and held a different spot in the squirrel pecking order. I watched with interest in the spring as the new crop of babies joined the squirrels and found their place in squirrel society.

One year there was a little squirrel born who had a rough time of it. The poor little guy tried to get to the feeder, but the other squirrels would chase him away with murder in their eyes. They wouldn't tolerate him within fifty yards of the feeder, and the only reason I ever came up with was that through some genetic fluke he was an albino squirrel. At last he gave up trying to live in the community that rejected him, and I found him living way back in the woods by himself.

It's sad, but human society, friendships, even families are not all that different. It seems that for many people the most serious offense you can commit is simply to be different from everyone else. The world has developed standards of normal behaviors that are based not on logic or reason but on simple herd mentality. If everyone else does it, it must be right. One of my friends in medicine tells his patients, when addressing the cardiac risk factors in their blood work, "Yes, Mr. Johnson, your levels are within normal limits . . ." and, oh, how the patient smiles until he continues ". . . normal, that is, in a country where it is normal to die of heart disease."

That, my friends, is our problem. We live in a country where the accepted and normal lifestyle, if followed, will normally result in death from lifestyle diseases. The average American is so pressured and stressed that free time has become a luxury they feel they can no longer afford. And we are not the only ones. As I travel the globe, I find the same thing is increasingly true everywhere. More and more demands on our time and our children's time rob us of the rest and the peace, not only in the lives of the adults but in whole families. To live at such a pace is harmful physically, but even worse is the inevitable spiritual death that comes from neglect. It is simply impossible to live the way most of us are living and have either time or inclination to seek after God and develop a relationship with Him sufficient for salvation.

I know, for I tried to live that life and find God at the same time, and let me assure you, if anyone could have done it, I would have achieved it. I am a hard worker and am disciplined and organized. Surely I would have a better chance than most, and all I found was bitter failure! At last Sally and I decided enough was enough. We would be albino squirrels, and we would live the life God intended for us to live, regardless of public opinion!

Let me share what we did and what some others have done. I am not dogmatic, nor do I want everyone to do things my way. My intent is to share what has worked and allow you, the reader, to adapt the principles I share to your own situation under the guidance and leadership of God, not Jim Hohnberger. We are all different individuals, and thankfully we have an individual God, not a "one size fits all." He adapts His ideals and plans for the individual, allowing us to become the very best we can be. So how did we start?

I believe most of us take a twenty-four–hour day and try to decide what we can possibly eliminate from it to slow down and simplify our lives. Unfortunately, this method doesn't work real well for most of us because most everything we do each day seems like a priority or we wouldn't waste our time on it. Sally and I decided to schedule our days around what we wanted to achieve, and then add the extras, and when the schedule was full, it was full. We had to discard those items for which we had no time left.

We wrote down our priorities:

1. Developing a walk with God that was real, vibrant, effective, and lasted all day.

While most of us would want this as our foremost goal, the time demands will vary from person to person. I wasn't working, and I knew I had a lot in my life that needed correction, so I devoted a lot of time to personal study and prayer when we first moved to the wilderness. But most people do not have that kind of time. The goal is connection with Christ, and as long as that is achieved, it makes no difference how long you spend on your personal devotions. Let the Lord lead. If you find you can't get well connected or that you are losing hold of Jesus as the day goes by, perhaps you need to readjust the time spent in this area. Regardless of how much time you spend in devotions, if you are not getting connected to God, the time is worthless. Connection is the key that unlocks the secret of the Christian life.

2. Working toward a marriage that had real spark and love while eliminating the hurtful patterns of behavior we had fallen into.

Relationships take time, and outside of your relationship with God, no other relationship has as much potential to influence your happiness and your salvation as your marriage does. Time invested here pays tremendous dividends and should be considered, in my humble opinion, more important than your work. If you call me at noon, you will get the answering machine because my girl and I are out in the swing visiting. Just the simple act of letting the machine get the call tells your partner they are more important than work.

3. Creating a family that really works, meaning a home where all members are bound tightly by love; an orderly home; and a place where the children and parents are learning self-control.

Closely related to this is the time spent as the family. Few things send a stronger message to me about a family than to call and be told, "Sorry, Jim, we will have to call you back. It's family time!" Family time is not just recreation though; it is taking the time to do the type of training that helps eliminate the need for discipline.

4. A lifestyle that allows time to think and act intellectually without the push, rush, and hurry that mark so many poor decisions.

We all have exactly the same amount of time in a day, and it is perhaps our most precious commodity. Like a high-pressure salesman, the devil tries to arrange circumstances so that the time available to contemplate the choices before us is as short as possible. The effect is that even choices that are seemingly small and insignificant can have major consequences. Take our words, for example. Most of us, thinking back over our lives, can find at least a time or two when someone's ill-considered words hurt us terribly, yet how fast we allow words to flow out that we can never recall. We must remember that we often do not see cause and effect, and our choice of what to say might be different if we take the time to consult the One who does see the end result.

5. Income adequate to meet family needs.

The notion of wresting a living from the land is romantic, and oh, so very appealing for those who want to get free of the system, but it is also very unlikely to come true. No matter how efficient the household, there are still things one needs a cash income to obtain. We must understand that the money in our pockets was traded to us for our time. If we are trying to redeem time for other purposes, then we must examine carefully just how much work is needed. While work should not rule us, we should also provide for ourselves, except under unusual circumstances. Christians should not expect either the government or the church to support them simply because they choose not to work.

What does this mean practically? For some this may mean working just a few hours a week if their earning potential is high, while another might need to work more than forty hours just to survive if they have limited skills or opportunity. Another common problem is that a skilled person will set out to run their own business and then charge less than they are worth, and then find themselves very much in demand but not very profitable. We should not be afraid to charge a fair price for services rendered.

6. Time for social interaction with others.

The human being came from his Creator with social needs, and these need a place in our schedules. The amount of interaction need not be large, but there should be some consistent contact with others. This not only provides enjoyment, but it helps us stay intellectually stimulated, not stale and closed minded.

You can see examples of how our schedule took shape in my book *Empowered Living*. But many people have said, "OK,

Hohnberger, you lived this lifestyle under unusual circumstances, and we already know you made it work for your family, but what about us? We live in the real world. Does this work when it hits reality face to face? What about busy professionals, working moms, or single mothers?" It's a fair question, isn't it? Let me introduce some families. They haven't all done what we did, but they have found a schedule to be a tremendous benefit.

Helen is a vibrant woman who always, she admits, kept a very neat and orderly house. On the surface it would seem senseless to profile someone so organized, but I think it is worth our time, for Helen is like so many of us who look so good to the outside observer and yet find frustrations and difficulties in their day that others seldom see. You see, Helen was organized after a fashion, but she admits she came to the end of her day and usually found she had not accomplished what she desired. So let's join her on an eventful day.

" 'Why, Danny, why?'

" 'It is just no good, Helen. I just don't want to continue this any longer.'

" 'Is it me or the kids?'

" 'No, you do a fine job with the children. It's just something with me! Goodbye, Helen.'

"I was heartbroken when my marriage ended, and so were my children. I never wanted a divorce, and yet I found myself with three children and no husband. The whole family used to rise early with Danny, and now I thought, *Well, at least we can sleep in,* but such are the plans of man, and God had other ideas. When you are the only one responsible for running your family, there is no one to blame if things don't get done, and many nights I found the day over and things still to be finished. People said, 'That's just how it is when you're a single parent.'

"*There's got to be a better way,* I thought. *But what?*

"When I sat down and looked at what I did every day, I soon discovered that we had no set time to rise, to eat, to go to bed, etc. It varied every day. *This is crazy,* I thought. *We ought to at least be able to eat at the same time every day, so I can plan.* And that's how I began. I started just by getting the basics of rising at the same time, eating at the same time, and going to bed at the same time in place. This may not sound impressive, but try it for a few days and you may find what I did. Suddenly, I had the beginnings of control over my life— over my time. We started getting more done! I was so excited, I added other areas to the schedule, such as set times for worship and set times for play. The more I scheduled my day, the better things went. I taught my children to take more responsibilities, and as they did so, I had more time to invest in them.

"I realize I am not the typical single mother because I don't have to work outside the home, and many have to. However, I know the principles of time management work, even if the only time you have available to control is in the evenings. I found that I could even find time for an afternoon nap with my two littlest ones, and what a blessing it is for a single parent. Those few minutes of rest give me the energy to invest in my family."

Fred and Florence were different in that their pressures came from trying to have it all and do it all. Fred is a successful business-man and, with Florence, had built quite a life for their family of two boys. They had been living in a three thousand-square-foot home, but the money was pouring in from the business, so they upgraded to a ten thousand-square-foot home, a six-car garage, and more toys than they had time to play with. In addition to the seven cars, there was a tractor, two jet skies, a motor home, and a second home at the beach. They also owned a very large house-boat. Fred and Florence had everything a human being could ever dream of to make them happy, and they still were looking for something else that would make life worth living.

They came to my meetings simply because their original plans for the weekend had fallen through, and after the first meeting, they just *had* to talk to me. Could my message work for them?

I spent two hours with them that day, and about the same amount the second day; and they set out to change their lives. I checked in from time to time, calling whenever I felt impressed, and I watched them begin to change. Fred cut back on his business and didn't service as many clients, but that was easy compared to rebuilding the family life.

"Jim," Florence complained, "you've got to understand what our home is like. I mean, the children get up and make their own breakfast of cold cereal and toast. I hate to admit it, but we used to let them eat in front of the television watching cartoons. I never, and I mean never, made a hot breakfast. I just wanted them to get done and out of the way so I could watch my TV program that came on later that morning."

"Well, Florence, there is no time like the present to make some changes." I smiled at her, but she seemed overwhelmed at the whole idea of getting up early enough to make breakfast. Still, she was willing to try, and if you ask her husband today, he will say, "We put out quite a spread for breakfast, and it's my job to make the fruit plate." The first items they changed were not very significant. They simply decided to get up in time to have worship and to have a specific time for the meals. These are not major items, but if you are like Fred and Florence and have never done it before, these things are huge accomplishments.

"We had never had worship in the morning, although we often had prayer at night before bed and sometimes a story," they admitted. When they set out to try and change, God honored that choice and gave them the ability to do what they had never before accomplished. It is that way with all of us. God never provides the strength and power before we need them. Until the choice is made to obey, what good would it do us?

Florence and Fred have continued to change and adjust their schedule. They still live in their huge home and work the same business. They dream of a home that is out in the country, but for now this is where they are, and they are making as many changes as can be made right now. They have freed time up to spend as a couple and have worked at beginning to communicate once more.

"It's so hard to stop the old habits," Florence commented. "Just the other day he did something that I felt was offensive. The Lord urged me to speak to him and explain my concerns. I found myself resisting. My old way of dealing with things was to just give him the silent treatment for a few days, but now I have to express my feelings. And while it is good, it is also very hard for me."

"We're doing better, Jim," Frank said with a grin. "We have scheduled our mornings and early afternoons. We even have the evening planned, but we are still trying to find a workable schedule for the late afternoon until evening."

"Great," I encouraged. "The process of change is gradual, and those who tend to succeed are those who go through the process systematically, a little at a time. You're on the right track." I have watched families whose major difficulties with each other stem from a lack of schedule, and it is easily solved. A few minutes with a sheet of paper to organize their lives and a determination to change in the strength of God are all that is needed. Well, almost all, because the other is an acceptance of the idea that you will be misunderstood and looked upon as an oddity by those about you. Like that albino squirrel, you may be garnering the hostility of those who just don't understand why you have to be so different from them. Don't worry too much about the reaction of others. Someday in heaven you may find that all your neighbors were albino squirrels too, and you'll be in good company!

CHAPTER 8

MR. HALF DAYS

But if any provide not for his own, and specially for those of his own house, he hath denied the faith, and is worse than an infidel (1 Timothy 5:8).

"Well, well, here comes Mr. Half Days." Paul, the owner of the real estate office I was working with, greeted me in the hallway. God had arranged this type of employment for me, had called me to it almost against my will, but after some days in the office I began to wonder if maybe this call from God had been a wrong number. I had worked so hard in the wilderness to gain control of my time, and when I agreed to go back into the work force I had done so with the understanding that I would control how much and when I would work, not the other way around.

We lived sixty miles from the office, and I wasn't willing to make the long drive more than once a week. Hence my days in town were hectic. I had to make all my phone calls for the whole week in one day. I had to check in with clients and follow up on land contracts and mortgage applications, as well as handle listings and advertising. Most businesses didn't open before nine, and that often delayed me. I tried to be out of the office no later than two-thirty in the afternoon so I could finish my errands in town and make the long drive home. Of course I had trouble reaching every attorney, banker, or client I needed to talk with in a single morning. As I played phone tag with different ones, my stress level would start to rise, and the temptation to give way to aggravation and frustration became stronger minute by minute until I felt as though I was wrestling with a physical entity. I had to be part of the work force now, yet I just had to keep control of my time. These two apparently opposing aims seemed to clash with each other.

As I headed up the North Fork Road, away from town and away from the phone, I was tired. The road followed the river northward, and I drove automatically, my thoughts struggling with the problems I had faced. And yet, almost imperceptibly, the stress and the tension melted away amid the familiar scenes of beauty. As my frantic pace of the day slowed, I once more heard the voice of God calling to my heart, and slowly new ideas came along with it.

"Jim, you came out here to gain a connection with Me, and you are becoming so driven to achieve your goals for the day that I can't get a word in edgewise. You've got to change, not what you're doing, but the way in which you do it."

"Lord, You just don't understand the situations I get stuck in. Did You see those guys today in my office, trying to come to terms? I could have settled that deal fairly and politely in three minutes, but they both got focused on money. I could just see the greed on their faces. They went back and forth for a whole hour. They wasted an hour of my time! They nearly ruined the deal—it almost fell apart right there over a few hundred dollars! I thought I was doing well to sit there calmly and not to tell them what I thought about them."

"You should have gone to the bathroom."

"I should've what?"

"You should have gone to the bathroom, Jim."

"Why? I didn't need to go."

"Yes, you did, Jim. You've no idea just how badly you needed to go to the bathroom."

"I don't get it, Lord. What does going to the bathroom have to do with anything—especially when I don't need to go?"

"What is in the bathroom, Jim?"

"There is a toilet and a washbasin. Lord this is ridiculous, why don't . . ."

"Is there anything thing else in there, anything at all?"

"Let's see . . . there's a small closet of cleaning supplies and paper products. What are you trying to get me to understand?"

"There is privacy, Jim. No one is going to disturb you there. There is peace and quiet amid the storm of upset emotions and uncontrolled passions. You can escape to the bathroom for just a few minutes and reconnect with Me."

Suddenly things seemed to make more sense. I decided right then and there to change the whole focus of my days in the office from getting work done to staying connected with God. It might seem obvious to you, but it was a real revelation to me. In exactly the same way God had retrained my time management at home, He was going to have to retrain my time management at work. Under this new philosophy, it no longer mattered if the clients wasted my time. It didn't matter if they threw away my nicely arranged deals. What mattered now was controlling Jim.

Soon I began taking five minutes at the end of every hour and just walking around the block, to slow down and reconnect with God. Strangely, the more time I took to make sure I was self-controlled, the more smoothly my work seemed to flow. I learned God's principles applied even to my work—and so will you if you decide you want to come to the quiet.

Employment is necessary for nearly all of us. Few have sufficient means to provide for their families outside of some type of employment, and yet in real estate and in ministry, I have watched family after family move into an area in which they have no ability to earn a decent living—at least make a living in their given career. These moves are almost always the result of hurried, emotionally driven choices and not the result of well-thought-out and carefully planned convictions. These families always face a crisis, and while some adapt and thrive, many face huge financial losses when they are forced to sell for less than they paid just to get back to where they came from. With their tails between their legs, they run back to the city cursing the day they ever heard of country living. The natural human tendency is not to blame their shortsighted and poorly thought-out decisions; the natural course is to feel they were deceived and that the country living experience is an error of the devil rather than a tool of God. I feel bad for any who find themselves in the position of such families and in sharing what I am in this chapter, I hope to help you avoid at least some of the pitfalls.

The first question everyone should ask themselves before moving to the country is, "Can we live within our means right now, right where we are?" If not, then logically, the work that lies nearest is to begin learning how to do that.

Once you are living within your means, then you must make an honest assessment of your skills and temperaments. Some people are not cut out to live in the wilderness. This is not a defect or something to be ashamed of; rather it is evidence that God made each and every one of us unique individuals, and while all might benefit from coming to the quiet, the issue of what that quiet will consist of is very different for each person. One person might have all they can do to live in a subdivision, while another would not be happy unless their home was accessible only by a difficult wilderness trail.

The major issue for all of us is time redemption. If you can earn forty dollars an hour, don't move where you can only earn ten dollars because, while you may get farther away into the country, you will have to work four times as many hours to earn the same income you are used to.

I know I am raining on many a person's parade, but loving concern for your welfare constrains me to point out that the number of successful home businesses are few, far fewer than you would think, and that for most the dream of a home business is not a reality and should not enter seriously into your plans unless you are already successful in running one. Home businesses require discipline and self-management to a degree that most people are just not capable of providing.

So if you want to move to a quieter location, desire an environment closer to nature and nature's God, where *do* you start? I will tell you right now, don't plan on moving to Montana. In spite of what my family has found here, Montana is not the "Salvation State." It is Big Sky country, and its economy tends to be poor, making it difficult for an unskilled person to earn a decent living. So if you cross out Montana, where do you go? Well, it is almost always best to start in your own backyard. In much of the country, a drive of as little as twenty minutes or so will dramatically alter the real estate options. There is a tremendous advantage to staying in an area you already know, the greatest of which is being able to keep your current employment. A relatively small country property just outside of the urban and suburban sprawl is where most families belong. There are some exceptions. If you live in a very large city, it may not be possible to get out into the country with any reasonable drive. And there are times when a well-meaning but misguided extended family is so opposed to the aims of the parents for the spiritual development of their children that they will try to subvert every effort the parents make to reform. Under these circumstances, there may be a need from the outset to consider relocation outside of the home territory.

The next question, once you have settled on the idea of relocation, is, "Does the property we are interested in have year-round access?" You may gain access to property from a local, county, or state road; however, even some government-owned roads are not maintained or plowed in the winter. Make certain you understand how you can get to your property before you buy. Better still is to visit the property in all seasons; then you will know if the road is passable. Other lands are accessible only by private roads, which raise all sorts of maintenance issues, especially in bad weather. If you must have access to your property through the property of another, make sure your access is a true, legal, deeded access. The friendly neighbor who has no problem with you using his property to get to yours may sell his land next year to someone who may forbid such usage. Only property that has public road frontage or has deeded access through other private property should be considered.

After access, the most pressing issue becomes water, and in some cases, water rights. Don't assume that because there is a river, stream, or spring on the property that it is yours to use. Water rights can be very complex, and if you don't understand them, you need a knowledgeable real estate agent or attorney to sort them out so you know what you are getting. The same is true of mineral rights, property lines, easements, and covenants, as well as zoning restrictions.

I remember one man who purchased his ideal country property and spent thousands of dollars putting in a well, septic tank, and foundation. Only after most of his savings had been invested in a new trailer to live in on his property did he discover from township officials that no trailers were allowed. Zoning officers are not evil, but it is not wise to run afoul of them. In general, they are reasonable public servants who are quite willing to answer any questions you have about building or improvements on any property within their jurisdiction. It is well worth the effort to make friends with the local officer. They usually have a wealth of information about every aspect of the area, and while they will not do you any extra favors, they can help you avoid many costly mistakes.

Sometimes the problem with a property is not evident from an inspection, but a talk with neighbors and others in the area can give you clues to things about your property that you may not want to deal with. For example, when you walked the property with the real estate agent or broker at ten o'clock in the morning, he may not have known about the dirt bike race course just over the hill that causes tremendous noise every weekend from noon until midnight. But the neighbors sure will! Maybe it's the shooting range or the toxic chemical dump over the hill or merely the chicken or pig farm that you can easily smell when the wind is just right. The real estate salesperson may not know that the basement floods in the spring thaw, but the neighbor across the street, who loaned the previous owner his sump pump, will know. What you have found may seem like an ideal wilderness location, and the idea of generator power sounds quite romantic until the only other resident across the hillside runs their generator late at night and the sound reverberates off your home till the windows rattle. There is no perfect property, although we would all like to find one. Realistically we take our ideal of perfection and have to work down from the ideal to what we are willing to compromise on. You might take less acreage or perhaps poor soil, maybe even a house that is a little too small or not quite what you want. As long as you are willing to let God lead, He will help you find the special place you need to be in, even if that place is right where you are now.

We must remember that the primary consideration of country living is to gain time for us to be true Christians and to safeguard our children from the world's influences. The more urban your setting, the more likely your family is to be exposed to all manner of evil in both sight and sound. Corruption and crime are not only reported but, in some cases, idolized. City life is increasingly artificial, and the values it teaches are incompatible with the principles of true Christianity. Excitement, gambling, and the constant whirl of activities tire the mind and body while the unhealthful environment imperils the well-being and allows the transfer of epidemic diseases.

One truth about wilderness and country living that takes people unawares is that in spite of the wonderful surroundings, people often have conflicts. The land may change, but people remain the same sinful creatures whether in the city or in the country. Some of these people may even be in your own church group, and the list of things people in the country can find to disagree on is endless. There are the issues of the use of natural versus artificial fibers in clothing, hand excavation versus using a backhoe, even the use of ATVs versus golf carts. These are just some of the lighter and more humorous ones. If you move to the country, you can plan on at least one person misunderstanding you.

In spite of all the trials and difficulties, if you apply yourself, you and your family will benefit immensely from coming to the quiet. Remember, the focus is not on the country living but on what we desire to gain from country living. This means facing ourselves and our problems, our shortcomings, and our faults. It means rebuilding those broken relationships with our family members or spouses. It means accepting that things are not always going to be easy.

I found this to be true when I set up my real estate practice in the North Fork. As I mentioned before, the environmentalists hated the very idea of a real estate broker in this pristine valley. For three years, they tore down every sign of mine they saw. People threatened us, but I persisted. I am not a poster boy for development, and if the environmentalists had listened, I could have shared with them the things I was doing in the North Fork that not only helped my clients but also helped the environmentalists achieve their goals. I knew the type of land the federal government was after, and when a property that met their requirements came up for sale, I did everything I could to see that the government was the purchaser. When a private parcel came on the market, I would visit the property owners on either side and let them know in case they didn't want a new home next to them. Often, one or the other and sometimes both would buy the property and secure it from development. I am pleased to report that in the years I sold real estate in the North Fork Valley, the number of privately held parcels actually declined by a significant number. As a realtor, I was not the enemy that the environmentalists feared I would be, but most still do not see the forest for the trees, and some would incorrectly blame me for development, which, had I not followed the course I did, would have been far more extensive.

I worked as Mr. Half Days for a number of years and became Coldwell Banker's number one real estate agent in northwestern Montana. I worked only a partial day once a week in the office, and yet God abundantly blessed me. And He is waiting to bless you. Your pathway will likely differ from mine in many particulars, except one. If you want heaven's blessing, you are going to have to learn to go through your days hand in hand with Jesus. Whether you can cut your work back to a half day or not doesn't really matter. Most of us will not be able to be Mr. Half Days. However, anything less than continual communion with God as you work will end in the same frustrating failure I found when I tried to go it alone. When I meet Jesus in the streets of heaven, I don't want Him to say, as did the owner of my brokerage firm, "Here comes Mr. Half Days." I want Him to say, "Here comes My Mr. All Day, Every Day, Each and Every Moment of the Day." This is the goal I am striving for. I believe it is your desire as well. Let us begin today!

CHAPTER 9

LIVING THE WILD LIFE

Neither shalt thou be afraid of the beasts of the earth (Job 5:22).

In the wilderness, the drama of life and death in our sin-scarred, damaged world is played out time and time again. Often it is our pleasure to witness the miracle of birth and new life among the wild creatures, but death also seeks them, and it had happened in our own yard.

I was upstairs working when Matthew, still a skinny preteen at the time, looked out the window at one of his favorite fawns and saw a wolf getting ready to attack her right in our yard. All I heard was Matthew's distressed voice screaming, "No!" I leaped down the stairs several at a time and saw the wolf and the deer and then Matthew heading out the door.

"No!" I called after him, in an eerie imitation of his cry, but it was too late to stop him as he charged out, determined to save the fawn. The wolf might have expected defensive behavior from the fawn's mother, but when Matthew charged it, waving his arms and yelling like a wild Indian, it paused. This strange two-legged creature didn't look like any mother deer it had ever seen, and the novelty of the situation seemed to win the day as the wolf backed off and left to find a meal Matthew wasn't guarding. I had made it outside, but it was Matthew who had driven off the predator and saved the baby!

The fawn was promptly named Baby Saved. It belonged to a large doe we called Friendly, thanks to her outgoing personality. Year after year, Friendly brought her fawns to see us, and to this day we almost certainly have deer on our property that are her descendants. Over the years we have befriended scores if not hundreds of wild animals, not by chance, but as a deliberately planned part of our life here in the wilderness.

In our move to the North Fork Valley, we had gotten rid of the television, videos, radio, practically everything artificial in the way of entertainment. It just made sense to us that we would make friends with all the little critters and determined that we would use patience and perseverance to attain this friendship without the use of chains, fences, or leashes. We placed a mineral block in our yard where the deer could get to it, and gradually they got used to our coming and going. As they got used to us we came closer, tossing them a little grain or a carrot, and bit by bit we lured them closer. Matthew was a champion deer tamer. Even though a young boy, he learned to be very patient, and as the deer moved closer, at last we could feed them by hand. After we had gained more of their trust, they let us pet their necks and rub their antlers. Finally they even approached us on their own.

We set up a feeding station for them and stocked it with grain. The barriers between wild animal and human being were broken down, and we were privileged to taste, even if just a little, life as it once was in Eden. We never fed them enough to stop their search for natural foods and the continual browsing that deer do. We knew they needed to graze to maintain their health. Interestingly, they remained nervous and uneasy about other human beings, as if they understood that we might be safe but others were not to be fully trusted. Baby Saved became so bold that she would walk up the three steps to our cabin and knock at the door with her little hoofs if she felt we were late in putting out grain at the feeder.

We also made friends with a deer we called Big Buck. He had a fantastic ten-point rack that many would have longed to hang on their trophy wall. In spite of his wonderful antlers, he became our most approachable buck, often coming silently, looking for his favorite snack food—wheat crackers. Big Buck seemed unique among the male deer population because he was willing to overlook the shortcomings of human beings and enjoy not only our food but our company.

In the last two decades, we have witnessed a steady stream of deer, some coming and some going, and on any given day we may have a dozen or more at the feeder. They have gotten used to us from one deer generation to the next, and some are so brave, they will eat out of the container as we try to refill the feeder. In the deer world, the bigger bucks rule, but in our yard it seemed the does, fawns, and younger bucks made out the best. They had less fear and came right up to eat while we stood beside the feeder, while the larger, more mature bucks stood off at the edge of the woods, jealously pawing at the ground, snorting, and carrying on. They wanted the grain so badly, but just not quite badly enough to risk human contact. It was torture for them to watch the other deer, normally so inferior to them, eat "their" grain.

Friendly had a radio collar placed on her by wildlife biologists. However, she was such a huge deer that even the large collar they placed on her had rubbed away the fur, and when she showed up in our yard, Matthew and Andrew were appalled to see their much-loved pet missing fur and her skin rubbed raw from the constant friction. The boys were ready to throw out all wildlife biologists right then and there. I explained that the biologists do an important and valuable job and I was sure if we spoke to them they would understand our concern.

Mike, the biologist, and his wife, did understand and decided to set up a net-enclosure trap in our yard so they could remove the old collar. "How long do you think it will be before the trap works?" he asked me.

"If I put out the food, she'll be here," I replied confidently. Friendly was used to feeding at our place, and she would come the moment food was set out, often eating right out of the bowl in our hands. Sure enough, Friendly showed up and walked right into the trap. But how to catch her was the next problem. I had never tried to catch a wild deer with my hands, but Mike couldn't do it alone, so I was about to receive some on-the-job training. We entered the little net-enclosed cage that had trapped her, and I grabbed her head.

Now I will tell anyone who might be foolish enough to want to duplicate my actions—don't! At that moment I thought I had grabbed a whole herd of deer. She let out frantic snorts, and four hoofs flew out as she braced herself, as though a mountain lion had grabbed her. The strength of a wild creature is quite astonishing. I was sure there had to be more than one deer in that hide. No matter how I tried, I couldn't wrestle her to the ground. Mike had the rear half, and together we still couldn't get her down. At last Mike's wife helped us, and the three of us just barely pinned her so the collar could be removed.

I was holding her neck, and she raised her head to me as if to say, "I trusted you. How could you?" With the collar removed, Mike warned me that letting go was even harder than grabbing hold. He demonstrated this just moments later. After his wife let go, he let go, and Friendly kicked him in a most unfriendly spot. Doubled up outside the enclosure, he urged me to hurry and let go before she caught her breath and really let me have it. If I could judge from Mike's pain, it looked like there was plenty of "it" even when she was tired. I couldn't imagine anything much worse than a sharp deer hoof to the groin.

I let her go, and she darted to the edge of the lawn, where she snorted and pawed the ground, giving me the worst deer scolding I ever heard. She was certainly letting me know what she thought about me. For weeks afterward, when she came to feed she would eat from Sally's, Matthew's, and Andrew's hands. But if I stepped outside, she would start to leave. It took a solid month before she lost her fear of me. I suppose I deserved it. No lady wants to be picked up without permission, and even tasty peace offerings did nothing to temper her anger for a good long while. Considering Mike's fate, though, I think I made out very well!

Through this meeting with Mike, my boys found a friend in someone who at first appeared to be an enemy. Mike opened the world of biology in a wilderness park for the boys. He invited them on projects, took them along to investigate grizzly bear kills, even let them go on plane trips to check on wolf packs. They learned in a way that nothing else could have taught them that one poorly considered action, like placing a collar too tight, does not a bad person make. Through Mike, they got to do things others only see on TV specials or just dream about. Isn't that the very best type of friend to have—one who opens new horizons before you and challenges your thinking so that you grow and develop into a more rounded person? No chapter on "living the wild life" could be complete without a thank you to all the fine and dedicated people like Mike, working to make sure our next generations enjoy the same wildlife we have.

For years, it seemed as if we were a real-life wilderness family, at peace with nature and each other, but God had led us out to the wilderness to do more than just enjoy ourselves, although I am certain that He loves for His children to be happy. He had led us here for our character development, and we would soon learn that no matter how close we had come to the way life was for our first parents, no matter how idyllic our setting, that sin had indeed come to Eden.

Family worship was becoming very special to us, and we had just gotten started one night when we heard *boom!* It was a gunshot, and very close! That day was opening day of deer-hunting season, and this shot, so close, unnerved us all. The boys were terribly worried about "their" deer, and in truth, so were Sally and I. We tried to continue worship, but a second blast put an end to that idea. How can you concentrate when someone is shooting at creatures you love? The boys and I decided to walk down toward the road where the shots had come from. We found two hunters who had stopped their car and were observing their kill.

"Big Nose!" the boys yelled and ran over to embrace the fallen creature that had breathed its last. I don't remember exactly, but the boys were probably around nine and eleven years old, and Big Nose had been a pet for three years. They burst into tears at the loss of their pet, while the two hunters just stared at them in wonder and shock. I just shook my head at them. I had hunted for years before becoming a Christian. I could tell by one look at their faces that they knew this had been an illegal kill. Big Nose was crossing the road to our place and had the bad timing to do so in front of them. They had actually shot her from the car. Never mind that bullets travel a long way if something doesn't stop them, or that another car could have driven into their line of fire, or, worse, another human being, a hunter walking back to his car along the road perhaps, might have appeared. Never mind that they were clearly near residences, with one visible just a little way off at the road side. All the safety concerns aside, I just couldn't understand how any hunter could consider it sporting to kill an animal from a car! There is no challenge, no skill required, and clearly no common sense needed for such an action.

Matthew and Andrew were livid and understandably so. Through their tears they told the men about the pet they had just slain. They wanted to take the hunting license numbers and report them, but, praise God, I was impressed that this was a time for growth and refused. Such action would not bring Big Nose back to life, and if these men were so ignorant of sportsmanship and fair play that even concern for their fellow human beings' safety did not deter their actions, then a fine would not, could not instill such values in them. I let them take the carcass, for there was nothing to be gained by retaining it except the possibility of another dead deer at the hands of these men. We left as they loaded up their trophy, and I wondered once more just what type of man could do such a thing. Back home, the boys grieved. This was their first face-to-face confrontation with the enormity of evil and sin, and they were ready to throw out all hunters as evil. It is a hard thing to love the sinner while hating the sin, and my children struggled with the very idea. They wanted to replay the scene in their minds over and over. I understood that memories are a natural part of the grieving process, but I also understood that their minds must be taught that Big Nose was gone and nothing was going to change that. The problem with going over something in our mind repeatedly is not just that it becomes impossible to move forward, but that the problem gets larger and more difficult every time we review it. Many people find themselves trapped in their own minds by thoughts that don't merit such attention.

I explained that hunters come in two varieties, good and bad, just like Christians in the church. They could be free of all their anger and unwanted upset feelings if they would yield them to God. It was a hard fight for them, one that took a couple of days until at last they gave up on hatred, revenge, and bitterness. We discussed the price of love and whether they wanted to keep paying it. They could stop feeding deer, stop making friends with them, and spare themselves the chance of deep and personal pain, for such things could happen every year. Or they could take the chance and reap the blessings. I was very pleased when they came to understand through this experience that, though love often hurts us, to love unconditionally and to forgive wrongs frees the soul. They learned to surrender to God the feelings they didn't want anymore, and the principle has served them to this day. Both have had others offend them over the years, and some have done things to the boys that to all human reasoning should have made them enemies, and yet they hold no animosity toward anyone, and at least in part, they have Big Nose to thank. Big Nose is long gone, but her sacrifice was not in vain, and we have come to see that all things really do "work together for good to them that love God, . . . who are the called according to his purpose" (Romans 8:28).

This is what we came to the quiet to accomplish. Our family was together, working through problems and difficulties with God. We were not free from the influence of evil, but it had ceased to be something ever before us, and thanks to this isolation, when the boys did come in contact with it, it appeared in all its ugliness and encouraged all of us to seek a closer connection with God that we might be freed from its clutches.

In the book *Escape to God,* I told a little about the boys' pet bear Lonesome, but such a grand and exciting pet deserves more than a fleeting mention. Lonesome had first come to our home with her family. She was one of the three cubs with the mother black bear that came to our house in answer to prayer. Her mother was the very bear that had come to the door and stood there face to face with Sally, showing my wife that God had freed her from her fear of these fantastic creatures. That fall the mother bear was shot by hunters, and the three cubs appeared in our yard, alone and bedraggled. We bought large amounts of wind-fall apples to try and fatten them up for the soon-coming winter; but without a mother to help them select a den site, their odds of survival were slim.

Our fears for them were well founded, and the next spring only one cub returned to us. She was as sorry looking as you ever saw. She came to our back door, and we felt so sorry for her, we gave her a plate of pancakes and maple syrup. Every morning after that, she was at the door. How could we refuse this poor lonesome thing that had lost her whole family! We fed her a little here and little there, and the name Lonesome just seemed to fit. Lonesome became like the family dog, always there, always glad to see us. She slept back in the forest just behind our property. Once, after getting up from a nap, she walked back to our home, where, unknown to her, we had guests. She was getting to be a good-sized bear by this point, and when she walked around the corner and headed right toward us, the visitors were scared to death!

Lonesome loved to spend time with us and would play with the boys on the swing set or in the sandbox. She trusted us, but only us. If she was napping on the back deck and heard a strange car in the driveway, she became a black shadow, calmly disappearing into the forest. It was a rare opportunity to interact with one of the largest of forest creatures. Lonesome had freely chosen human companionship, so it seemed doubly tragic some three years later that she died almost identically to Big Nose—an illegal shot from a car on the North Fork Road. A friend of ours witnessed the event and asked the hunters, "Why?"

"We want a bearskin rug to go in front of the fireplace," one answered.

Ironically, Lonesome, the gentlest and friendliest of bears, died so that someone could display her head and skin as an example of a dangerous creature whose threat the hunter's "bravery" had removed from the wilderness. Our friend, sick at heart over what he had just seen, came and told us of our bear's fate, and it snuffed the happiness out of our day. We talked about it as a family, prayed about it, and we will never understand why the Lord allowed this tragic ending for Lonesome. Perhaps in her later years as her own health failed, she might have been a danger to us, but that is pure speculation. In truth, such tragic things happen all the time in our world of sin. Accidents and illnesses rob the lives of those we love. Only in eternity can we really begin to understand the "why" behind all the events that trouble and sadden us.

Yet even in grief and sadness, nature teaches us heaven's method of dealing with the problems of sin. How much animals grieve over the loss of loved ones, it is impossible to know. Certainly they are affected to some degree, but they seem to understand instinctively that life holds too many opportunities for happiness and productivity to allow gloomy thoughts to prevail for very long. In place of a tree toppled by the wind, new ones spring up, and in place of sadness over pet loss come the joys of new pets found.

In our area the coyotes took a very heavy toll on the rabbit population. In fact, many of the moderate-sized predators seemed to view rabbits in the same way human beings see a fast-food restaurant. One spring morning the boys found a baby rabbit without a mother and adopted it. They fed it with an eyedropper and made a snug little home for it in a box, which they kept under the bed. It didn't take the little creature long to thrive, and it didn't take us long to discover that rabbits like to be active at night. They are nocturnal feeders, and as soon as the little fellow discovered how to get out of the box, it found all sorts of ways to cause mischief at night. However, after getting into things, it usually found its way to one of their pillows and slept snuggled close beside them the rest of the night. When it was big enough, we let it go in the yard, and it produced a large family. (Do rabbits ever produce anything else?) The offspring were surprisingly domesticated. Somehow, in whatever way rabbits communicate, it was passed on to each new generation that we were OK, as far as human beings go, that is, and I must admit it is nice that they don't run from us.

This experience set the stage for a more trying exercise in wilderness baby-sitting, when the boys located three baby Columbia ground squirrels, orphaned by a coyote or a wolf. The name "ground squirrel" is used loosely for a number of rodents in the squirrel family. In North America, the name also refers to a number of creatures, including chipmunks, prairie dogs, marmots, and woodchucks. The Columbia ground squirrels live in extensive underground burrows and in my area are referred to as gophers, although because "gopher" is a name more commonly applied to burrowing rodents of a totally different family in most places, I will refer to them here as squirrels.

These three babies—Sam, Sandy, and Sleepy—were very cute, and the eyedropper got a workout as the boys now had three hungry bellies to keep satisfied. Evidently the boys did well for these little babies because the squirrels quickly decided the boys were their parents and bonded to them. We gave them free run of the house, and they loved to run up our legs. Like any wild squirrel, they delighted in finding the highest spot to perch, which in this case was our heads. I don't know if I can blame them for my hair loss, but I know that being used as a climbing post put some real strain on the roots! What a blessed feeling to have tiny little feet climbing up your body, knowing that this must have been what it was like in the world before sin, when all the animals were friendly and unafraid.

Like any good parents, the boys took them out to the sandbox so they could learn to dig. They loved to tunnel, but it must be a skill learned by parental instruction because their tunnels always collapsed on them. We tried to confine them in a fence, but the hawks and ravens started eying them as easy meals, so we discarded that idea. They were always into mischief and so fast that their very quickness was a problem among us much slower human beings. Unfortunately, one died under someone's foot when it got under its descending path. Another met its fate when it tried to beat the closing door and only tied it in the race to the doorjamb.

Sam was the sole survivor, and we were desperate to get him to the wilderness before he met a similar fate. Sam at last found an unused gopher hole, with a large rock nearby for sentry duty. He adapted well to his new life, although he still came to the front door for snacks. The boys got to experience every phase of parenting through their wild little friends—love, caring, death, and even letting go! Soon Sam was running up and down the forty-foot hill into the meadow below us to meet with others of his kind. It was nice to see him learning to be a ground squirrel. Eventually he found a mate, and she didn't want to live by the house, so he left for the meadow and was out of our lives.

When people come to visit, we laugh and tell them we watch "Channel One"—our large feeding platform for the birds that provided endless enjoyment for decades. Every time we looked out, every mealtime in winter or summer, the birds were there. Hummingbirds came all summer, their tiny bodies and humming wings teaching that a hum in nature was not something to be neutralized with bug spray, but an announcement of the arrival of a gaily wrapped package. We like to think of creatures like the hummingbird as being untouched by sin, but even there in a beautiful package that weighs little more than a coin in your pocket are a variety of personalities and behaviors. Some birds are selfish and spend huge amounts of energy keeping others away from the feeders. Sally and the boys felt so bad at times, they would chase the troublemaker away with a broom! In those little ways the boys learned the need of justice. They saw that sometimes force must be used to defend freedom for all, and they saw it in a way that no book could ever teach.

Television can be used to baby-sit children, to entertain, and even sometimes educate, but it can never be what nature can and will be to any child who has the chance to experience it, and that is as a friend. Once friends with nature, the child begins to see the whole world as their backyard, and it opens to them almost unlimited ideas for adventure. They can set out and try great adventures and big expeditions, dream huge dreams, and you can join with them. It was just this love of nature that motivated the boys a few years ago to do some backpacking at Nasakoin Lake.

We have trained them as long as they can remember in the rules of camping in grizzly territory. They knew how to keep themselves neat and not even spill food on themselves while eating. They kept food well away from their camp and hung it where bears couldn't get it. After setting up camp by the lake, they followed all the normal precautions and went contentedly to bed. In the middle of the night, they found themselves suddenly awake. Outside the tent there were heavy footsteps, and on the other side of less than a millimeter of nylon came a low sound of *huhhhh, huhhhh, huhhhh*—the breathing noise of a grizzly at very close range. They nudged each other and held a short whispered prayer session about what to do. Clearly the bear was investigating their camp, and the tent offered little but the illusion of safety. At last they decided they had to get to their bear mace canisters. Taking what they thought might be their final breath, they unzipped the tent and clambered outside.

The bear backed off, but they could still hear it moving out in the darkness. Few things are more disconcerting than the knowledge that a large bear is interested in you and is wandering about your camp. The boys built a fire and kept it burning for a couple of hours before deciding the bear had moved on. They returned to their tent and with prayer, fell back to sleep.

When they returned home, their story caught my attention, for I had planned to go to that very location for what I refer to as my Enoch time, when I go off to spend some time alone with God in the wilderness and no phone or visitor can interrupt.

When people hear where I live, one of the first concerns they have is bear attacks. It is true that grizzlies are large and dangerous animals? The only reason I do not fear such an attack is that I am here at God's leading, and unless He allows it, nothing can harm me.

My family was hiking between upper and lower Kintla Lake, where the trail enters a lovely valley, maybe a hundred acres in size, dotted here and there with brush and small aspen trees. It is one of the most beautiful spots I know, with majestic views of multiple waterfalls pouring off the glacier above. The trail drops down into the valley before heading up the mountain to the upper lake. As we started through the valley, we startled a grizzly feeding in the aspens. The bear charged, as grizzlies will do, and all of us responded by freezing. I think it was Matthew who was carrying bear mace, and he dropped his hand to his mace canister, although it hadn't cleared the holster before she stopped at a range of about twenty-five feet, growling menacingly, popping her teeth, and huffing at us. Deciding she had taught us to keep our distance, she departed—just like that. But was it really just like that? No, the God we serve nudged her along.

Events like these had flooded my thoughts when I arrived some months later in the same location the boys had camped. I immediately saw why they had been troubled. The area by the lake was clearly a transitory path for grizzly bears over the range, and the boys had unwittingly camped astride the bear's right-of-way. I looked about, and some distance from the lake, raised well above it, I found a spot among some boulders to make my camp. It wasn't much of a spot, hardly large enough for my tent, but it was certainly not a place that bears were likely to roam. I enjoyed my evening and retired ready for a good night's sleep.

Somewhere between three and four that morning I awoke, just as the boys had, very aware of a large animal walking near my camp. Immediately I thought, *It's a grizzly bear!* I reached for my mace, but in the quiet of my thoughts God said, *"Jim, you don't need to worry about it. Let Me take care of it."*

"Lord, I know You can do anything, but I also know there is a grizzly bear out there. There shouldn't be, in these rocks, but there is. Perhaps it is the very bear the boys ran into. Maybe it has found food from others who have camped and thinks that human beings mean food."

"Jim, let Me take care of it."

I can't tell you how hard it was to hear those noises and not do something. God was stretching me, teaching me how to let reason rule over emotions, and how to trust Him even when I knew what the danger was. At last, the sky started to brighten. I had surrendered my ideas to God and was feeling calm and at peace when the Lord told me, *"You can look now, Jim."*

I wasted no time. I had pictured this bear as the mightiest of the mighty. You know how it is when you can hear danger and not see it—you always imagine it much larger than it really is. Now I was going to see this brute. I unzipped my tent and looked out at the monster and couldn't help laughing. I felt like the biggest fool in the world. I had spent hours worrying about a mule deer!

God had used the situation to guide and direct me, and this is what He desires for all who come to the quiet. God never promises it will be easy or an experience free from grief. He does hold out before you a little taste of Eden and the opportunity to grow in your trust in Him. You, too, can fall in love with nature as we did. Come to the quiet and live the wild life. You will never regret it, and it will fill your family's memories with happy, heart-warming stories that will in turn inspire a whole new generation to come to the quiet.

CHAPTER 10

I LIFT UP MY VOICE

And I saw another angel fly in the midst of heaven, having the ever-lasting gospel to preach unto them that dwell on the earth, and to every nation, and kindred, and tongue, and people, saying with a loud voice, Fear God, and give glory to him; for the hour of his judgment is come: and worship him that made heaven, and earth, and the sea, and the fountains of waters (Revelation 14:6, 7).

Sales, like most professions, requires periodic continuing education. One time in my early career I attended an advanced sales school in Madison, Wisconsin. I hated to go to those things, first of all because I didn't follow all the typical sales gimmicks, and second, I wanted to be home with my family, not in a lonely hotel room. I had learned to make sure I requested a single room because I definitely didn't fit in with much of the crowd that attended such gatherings, and sharing a room made things very difficult. The guys were as nice and outgoing as any group of salesmen you could hope to meet, but they saw this time as an opportunity to party and drink, which put me almost completely out of step because of the values I had embraced as a conservative Christian.

So my mind-set upon arrival at the hotel was that this was something I had to endure for my career and I would make the best of it. At least with a single room, I could sleep while everyone else had a "good time." You can imagine my shock upon finding someone already settled into my hotel room. I thought there must have been a mistake, but the hotel assured me that there was no other room and that Mike and I would have to get along as best we could.

No two people sharing a room could have been more different. Mike would go out drinking with the guys only to drag himself back to the room hours later. He usually came in to find me reading my Bible. I don't know if the alcohol loosened his tongue, but he started asking me questions, and we'd talk every night about the Bible, God, and religion. By the end of the week, he had become interested in my religion, and I put him in touch with a church in the Chicago area, where he began studying.

Time passed, and we moved to the wilderness. One day I got a call from Mike. He was going to be baptized and he really wanted us to be there if it was possible. It was a hard request to refuse, so we came back east. Right there in the church before the baptism, the pastor asked us to share about the things we had been doing and what our family had gained from our time in the wilderness.

Our presentation was not the well-thought-out presentations we share today; rather, it was a sketchy outline when we were just beginning to catch a glimpse of where God was leading us. For some reason the people liked what we had to say. There was a couple's retreat going on, and they asked if we would come and share our story with them the next evening. One couple, Chris and Margaret, came to see us afterward and asked if they could come and stay with us. "We're having marital problems," they confessed. They would become the very first family to ever come and stay in our home. We had no knowledge of marital counseling, only knowledge of God and what He could and would do for those who would let Him. Yet, they left us with a new beginning, direction, and hope for their future.

Another couple we met on the trip to Mike's baptism came to visit in the wilderness, and their time with us transformed their life, their marriage, and their children, as it did for the next family that visited. Pretty soon we were getting invitations to speak here, there, and everywhere! It was pretty amazing to us, but it was the beginnings of our ministry. We were discovering that God never blesses any human being with knowledge, skills, or experiences that can benefit others and then allows them to keep these to themselves. We have found something very special in the mountains—a practical experience in learning how to walk with God in similar fashion to what Enoch enjoyed, and Enoch was called out by God from the mountains of his home to reach out to the multitudes in desperate need of his information.

Enoch, I believe, was a simple preacher, who shared what worked in his life and encouraged others so that it could work in theirs as well. This was a great encouragement to us because this was how we shared with others. It wasn't fancy presentations or charisma that drew people to the message. It certainly wasn't our complex theological understandings that kept the invitations to our family coming. It was the changing lives of those who grasped what we were trying to say that made others want what we had shared with their friends. One time we gave a full seminar at a Methodist university, which had been billed incorrectly as a Wilderness Survival seminar. Let me assure you that the people attending this meeting sure didn't plan on the type of message we gave, but they loved it anyway! We talked about a different kind of survival.

At last, after I had worked many years in real estate, the Lord asked me to minister for Him in a full-time capacity. I don't mind telling you, I was scared! I had no idea how things were going to work out. Yet in stepping forward to minister to the needs and pains of others, I found not only that God provided me with skills to do the job He had called me to do, but I fell, almost without realizing it, passionately in love with what I do. All the things that once mattered—prosperity, promotions, popularity, praise, recognition, and reward—have been replaced by something far better.

I used to love studying God's Word. Now I love to find Him in His Word.

I used to pray before my day. Now I commune with Him throughout my day.

I used to know a lot about Him. Now I know more of what He knows about me.

I used to ask for guidance. Now I sense His hand upon the reins of my life.

My soul thirsts for a living God (see Psalm 42:2). I have determined that I will not back up, let up, or shut up until I have preached up, prayed up, stored up, and stayed up the cause of my God! I have a passion for my work because I have a passion for God.

God has a passion for me as well, and He has formed our ministry. We could never have envisioned all that has happened, from seminars and tapes to family camp meetings all over the country, and on to radio ministry, television appearances, articles, and books. Still more exciting opportunities await us.

Every one of us needs this passion for God if we are to obtain anything other than ordinary religion, which usually fits people to miss out on the pleasures of sin while never removing sin's control over them. They have enough religion, and only enough religion, to be miserable in this life and unfit for the next. This is all religion can do for a person—unless they fall passionately in love with God. Then things can change.

The problem with being passionately in love with God is that suddenly you find yourself out of harmony with those who also claim to be seeking Him. In many ways, those who most oppose true religion are the most zealous proponents of having the right doctrines and implementing all the right reforms, while adamantly refusing to take the final step of falling in love and offering up their hearts to God. Good, well-meaning church members who claim to love God and desire to see Him return become awfully mad if I suggest the simple biblical truth that as Christians we have an opportunity to hear God's voice to our hearts, guiding and directing our actions. Why do so many turn their backs on the wonderful opportunity to know God, as it is their privilege? They do so because they fear what a real living connection to the God of the universe may cost them. Is that holding you back today?

I can list all the things God has asked me to give up over the years—from my cigarettes, my old ambition to succeed, right up to my many vehicles and large home. Yet, I know that not one of those things has ever brought me the pleasure I have gained from giving them up. Paul understood this and told us so in Philippians 3:8: "Yea doubtless, and I count all things but loss for the excellency of the knowledge of Christ Jesus my Lord: for whom I have suffered the loss of all things, and do count them but dung, that I may win Christ."

Every great man and woman in God's cause has come to understand this truth: Moses; Caleb and Joshua; Deborah; Hannah the mother of Samuel; David and Jonathan; Elisha; Daniel and his three friends Hananiah, Mishael, and Azariah; Haggai the prophet; Esther; and Nehemiah; even Nebuchadnezzar, the monarch of Babylon, learned at last the lesson that true greatness consists in true goodness—true godliness. And the New Testament is filled with more great men and women who chose to have a passion and love for God, in spite of great dangers and almost insurmountable problems.

The list of God's great men and women was not closed at the end of Bible history. Some names are known to us, but many of perhaps the greatest are known only to God Himself, having given their last full measure of devotion to Him whom they loved in death. No record but heaven's survives to bear witness of their bravery.

The Reformation brought with it men such as Wycliff, Huss, Jerome, Tyndale, Luther, and Wesley. Yet these men who were God's great champions were not the cause of the Reformation's success. It succeeded because ordinary men and women embraced its principles, and they transformed their lives and homes. So it has been with every reform and every effort God has made to uplift the human race from the depths of sin and suffering to which we have fallen. There may be leaders noted by the pages of history, but it is the average man and woman whom heaven marks as great because they acted—surrendered and cooperated—with God. They may have been seen by their fellow men as the weakest of the weak, but God shall account them great.

Who will be the great one of God who leads the reformation in your home, in your family? Must your little ones languish because something else, anything else, is more important? Your mission field of the home may seem tiny and insignificant, and yet it is the task to which the God of heaven has called you. Will you respond to His summons? Will you cast aside all else that your family might be saved?

Throughout this book, I have invited you to *come to the quiet,* both the literal quiet of the unhurried natural world and, much more importantly, the quiet of your own secret place with God. If you do, I promise that the opportunity to share with others will be placed before you by God, who desires that all should gain this experience. There is a need of a new generation today to pick up the standards of the Lord and advance them boldly before the kingdom of darkness, that there may be a shining light in the world pointing the way to come to the quiet, to escape to God, and to be empowered to live our lives totally for the benefit of other people. It is not a fanciful dream, my friend, but a living and breathing reality, awaiting only your decision to bring this experience into your life, your marriage, and your family.

If you do this, Satan's wrath will know no boundaries, and he will work to destroy you and the work you have been doing. Our enemy is a master planner. He has ways prepared to attack us that develop so gradually, the human being rarely understands that the events that seem to sweep over us by apparent chance are really part of his carefully orchestrated plots.

God allows these attacks from Satan for our character development. Too often we perceive the Christian life as one of ease and prosperity, but God "trains His workers by bringing to them disappointments and apparent failure. It is His purpose that they shall learn to master difficulties. Often men are tempted to falter before the perplexities and obstacles that confront them. But if they will hold the beginning of their confidence steadfast unto the end, God will make the way clear" (Ellen G. White, *Prophets and Kings*, 595).

God never gives special gifts or experiences so that they can be hoarded and kept to oneself. With His blessings always come opportunities to share. Over the last two decades we have shared our life story and how we came to know God with thousands of people. Tens of thousands more have heard our story on tape, on the radio, or on television, and many of these dear people would like to come and visit with us. Unfortunately, we are unable to accommodate but a handful.

Sally suggested that we hold an open house. We couldn't have that many people to camp on our small property, but almost unlimited space was available in the national forest and park. We would open our property to anyone who wanted to visit with us from 10:00 A.M. until 6:00 P.M. every day for a week. People could visit our home, raft the river, and climb a mountain or tour Glacier National Park. We liked the idea so much that we decided to make it an annual event to take place the last week in July every year.

So join us, as my family lays plans to open our house to the hundreds who have expressed an interest in coming and tasting, if only for a short period of time, this special place we call home, which has nurtured us and acted as the nursery for our personal experiences with God and the worldwide ministry this experience has spawned. We know that God has led in this development, and we are praying that countless families will make the hard choices that will transform and empower their lives.

CHAPTER 11

THE BIG BLOW-UP

My soul, wait thou only upon God; for my expectation is from him
(Psalm 62:5).

It is important for Christians to realize that we do not live in a vacuum but are citizens of an ever-changing and degenerating world. The wilderness may seem to be untouched by man, yet you will see that even the mighty forests bear the mark of sinful man.

In the late winter of 1910, the spring melt had come early and the normal rains never materialized. In their place came days of blazing heat and wind, combined with low humidity that drew what moisture remained right out of the Northern Rockies. July 15 brought storms filled with wild lightning and rain. The bone-dry air absorbed the rain long before it reached the parched ground, in a textbook example of a dry lightning storm. As the lightning touched and re-touched the earth, it left a trail of fire.

Early August showed somewhere between 1,700 and 3,000 fires burning across Idaho and western Montana, most of which foresters managed with relatively little equipment and manpower to contain or at least control. Not all the blazes were lightning strikes. Fires of human origin burned in many places, sparked by everything from trains to careless loggers. Nevertheless, by August 20 most would have said the worst was over.

That afternoon, it was another story. The winds swept in from Washington State like a hurricane, and in an instant the fires of

Idaho and Montana, which had seemed docile and dwindling, became raging firestorms that swallowed whole hillsides in a single gulp and then joined to form one huge conflagration, racing eastward on the wings of a seventy-mile-per-hour wind. It may have been the largest forest fire ever seen in American history; no one knows for sure. What we know is that throughout the night of August 20 and through the next day and the following night, the fire burned through three million acres. Whole towns were incinerated, and rumors flew that this was the end of the world. Sadly, for eighty-six people it was.

We should never underestimate the hatred the devil has for us all and how he rejoices when God allows him to bring disasters and with them, a harvest of unprepared souls. I will not linger on the morbid, but the danger is real to every one of us. Not one of us knows whether this day we hold in our hand is the last that will ever be ours. Therefore we must keep in mind that it is not just when we see obvious danger before us but also in times of peace and safety that we have a fragile and precious gift and death can strike unexpectedly at any one of us.

Edward Pulaski was one who saw the danger. He had prospected the Northern Rockies for more than two decades and, at the time of the great 1910 fire, was ranger of the Coeur d'Alene National Forest, having become a ranger just two years earlier. He and some of his men were trying to fight the fire on August 20. Realizing it was foolhardy to try and fight the blow-up during the evening wind storm, Pulaski tried to gather his men and managed to collect about forty-five of them and lead them on a mad dash for survival.

The winds were ripping whole trees from the ground. Sometimes a flaming tree would be cast on the wind a considerable distance, and for every tree so treated, scores of others lay crisscrossed in fallen heaps on the forest floor. This considerably changed the appearance of the landscape, and only someone with the intimate knowledge of the area that Pulaski had gained from prospecting could have known where to go. The nearby War Eagle Mine had two tunnels, and Pulaski led his men on a race with death for the longer tunnel. Smoke obscured everything, and the fallen and falling trees made travel in any direction almost impossible. One man was killed by a falling tree en route, while still another lingered too long and was caught by the fire and burned alive.

"We reached the tunnel just in time," Pulaski reported when it was all over. "I ordered the men to lie face down upon the ground and not dare sit up, unless they wanted to suffocate, for the tunnel was filling with fire, gas, and smoke."

The fire swept over their shelter, and the mine timbers caught alight, but Pulaski stood at the entrance informing anyone who might think of leaving that he would shoot them. Then, using his hat as a bucket, he fought the flaming timbers with mine water. "The men were in a panic of fear, some crying, some praying. Many of them soon became unconscious from the terrible heat, smoke, and fire gas. I too, finally sank down unconscious. I do not know how long I was in this condition, but it must have been for hours."

At five o'clock in the morning, fresh air finally filtered into the mine, and the men roused. "We tried to stand up, but our legs refused to hold us so we dragged ourselves outside to the creek to ease our parched throats and lips. Our disappointment was terrible when we found the stream filled with ashes and the water too hot to drink. We counted our number. Five were missing. Some of the men went back and tried to awaken them, but they were dead. When walking failed us, we crawled on our hands and knees. We were in a terrible condition, all of us hurt or burned. I was blind, and my hands were burned from trying to keep the fire out of the tunnel. Our shoes burned off our feet, and our clothes were in parched rags." In that condition, somehow Pulaski's party negotiated the burnt and still scalding terrain into the town of Wallace, Idaho. Pulaski survived and was later credited with inventing or at least refining the tool that bears his name, the "Pulaski"— half ax, half hoe—used by forest firefighters to this day.

The fire became known as the Big Blow-Up. As the smoke drifted across the country, darkening skies all the way to the east coast, even preventing ships from sighting stars as much as 500 miles out into the Atlantic Ocean, the traumatized nation and Congress addressed the issue of forest fires and for the first time decided to spend federal dollars on fire suppression.

Every able-bodied man in that area of the country was soon working the fire. Miners, loggers, settlers, even skid-row bums were packed on trains and sent in. The men got twenty-five cents an hour, a bedroll, and grub. The effort was praiseworthy, but it was the fall rains and snows that killed the fires. Human effort, no matter how heroic, has but little effect upon such a huge fire.

Realizing this truth, the forest service decided that fires must be attacked as soon as they were discovered and still small enough to control. Over the years, this evolved into the aim of all fires being extinguished by 10:00 A.M. the day after they are reported. Not that this happened overnight. Large fires occurred in the 1920s, but by the 1930s efforts at firefighting were becoming increasingly successful. After World War II, men and ex-military machinery attacked wildfires as never before, transforming the woods. Forests became denser and denser still. Areas that might have once had as few as three dozen trees per acre might become crowded to 3,000 trees an acre. Trees deprived of necessary light and nutrients died in the understory, while insects attacked and destroyed mature trees, leaving them dead, dry, and still standing. Dead wood built up on the forest floor, so that when fires did occur, they burned hotter and started crowning more often—racing through the tree-tops.

Gradually attitudes toward fire suppression changed once more. Facing forests that had become literal tinderboxes, officials now confronted the problem of removing excess fuels either by using "controlled burns," or allowing loggers to do it, or facing huge, almost uncontrollable fires. A controlled burn ran out of control in Los Alamos, New Mexico, a few years ago, burning more than 200 homes. That soured the public on the idea of controlled burns, yet almost every attempt to introduce logging has invited long and hostile disputes and even lawsuits from environmentalists, who feel that any logging is bad and are suspicious that "fuel removal" is just another word for clearcutting.

My degree is in forestry, so I was not blind to the physical problems besetting the beautiful area in which we chose to live. However, it is hard to consider these problems as a significant factor when the individual is for the most part powerless in the struggle between the environmentalists, the government, and the logging industry.

You too are going to find yourselves trapped one day in a situation in which you feel completely powerless, whether it is by political change, economic downturn, or natural disaster. Not one of us is immune to the assaults of the devil—just look back at history. Are you right now taking the steps that will enable you to stand with your faith firmly rooted in God when such events overtake you? Have you begun exercising faith in the "little" areas of life, learning how, through the power of God, to overcome sin and self in your own life? Have you come to see the hand of God even in the misfortunes and problems of your day-to-day life? If we lose our self-control over a flat tire or a child spilling juice, what will happen to us should the Lord allow even greater trials to come upon us?

God wants to make each one of us aware that He is leading and ordering the events of our lives and that nothing happens in our lives, no matter how difficult or trying, without His permission. He allows these things for our benefit, and while He does not cause problems and temptations, He does allow the devil to try us that we might be purified. It sounds nice and easy when we speak of this process in the abstract or when we talk of it happening to someone else. It is easier to think about difficulties coming to us in some distant future and not the here and now. That's what I did when we moved to the North Fork Valley. Yes, I knew there were dangers, but God had led us to the mountains, so surely He would take care of us. I put the possible problems out of my mind. I did not know that during one recent summer, my faith in this idea of divine watch-care would face its supreme test.

We have found that whenever we set out to do anything for God, Satan is aroused to attack us and try to prevent anything from happening that will encourage the subjects of his kingdom to seek God. Ever since we started to work for God, we have had all manner of attacks on our words, our personalities, our understanding of truth, our characters, even on our children. We thought Satan had done his worst in the past, but as any student of history might have been able to tell us, the pieces needed to destroy us were in place. I didn't know this test was coming, and perhaps it is just as well. Would I have kept my courage if I had known all the trouble that was about to transpire?

CHAPTER 12

TRIAL BY FIRE

When though passest through the waters, I will be with thee; and through the rivers, they shall not overflow thee: when thou walkest through the fire, thou shalt not be burned; neither shall the flame kindle upon thee. For I am the LORD thy God, the Holy One of Israel (Isaiah 43:2, 3).

It had been a hot summer day with a fantastically blue sky. However, when I stepped out my back door that afternoon I knew something was dreadfully wrong. To the north and to the south the sky was the same beautiful blue, but directly overhead smoke obscured the sky, not just over my house but trailing far off over Glacier National Park. Sally and I stood outside watching as ash, some of it still containing live embers, drifted down on us like snow. I got in the car and drove up Wedge Canyon.

About nine miles from our home, I found the fire. It was demonstrating what the professionals call extreme behavior, and flames rose hundreds of feet in the air. Already about fifty acres were burning in just the first four hours, and it was expanding rapidly. Clearly this fire was going places, and, like a loaded gun, it was aimed directly at our home.

Saturday morning brought no improvement in the situation. The west wind continued, and we learned the fire had grown to 350 acres overnight. By Saturday night the fire had almost doubled to 650 acres—more than one square mile! Overnight, the fire blossomed into 1,000 acres, and we realized at the current rate of expansion, our property would be hit as early as Monday night.

Preparing your property to survive a forest fire involves more than turning on sprinklers; it involves making the area surrounding your home uninviting for the fire. Homes are lost because of the materials used in their construction and because of ladder fuels that feed the fire to the structure site or into the surrounding trees and then to the structure. Ladder fuels are anything that allows the fire to move up from the ground into the upper level of the forest or house. Small trees, low hanging limbs, bushes, windfalls, and brush, even wooden decks can act as ladders for a fire. The goal is to remove these items up to a height of six feet. When it's done properly, the land resembles a city park, a clean area with large trees but no low limbs.

Our home was built of flammable logs, but the roof was metal, which was good with all the live embers drifting down upon us. No large overhanging decks invited embers to ignite under them. Still, our property was not prepared as it should be. My son Andrew and his wife, Sarah, came up early Sunday morning, and we got started on the task, but it seemed overwhelmingly large. We worked hard all day to complete all of about a quarter acre.

In spite of the frustratingly slow progress and the seemingly hopeless task, Sally and I were not discouraged. All that we had and all that we are had been surrendered to the Lord, and if He chose to remove our home or property, we trusted that He knew best. We knew that we had to do our part as well, and this we strove to do, but not trusting in our own efforts, for the first day showed us that our abilities were puny at best in the face of this great danger. If our home was to be spared, it would be because our God had, in mercy and loving kindness, intervened in our behalf.

Do you sense dangers ready to engulf your family? Are you working and putting forth real effort to protect them from the evils that threaten? Like us, you may need to do some serious pruning. Perhaps there is a need of finding a more sheltered location. As trees are more vulnerable to fire when too close together, so are our families when we allow them to remain in a dangerous situation or exposed to harmful influences. Brush feeds the fire to the larger trees, and so, too, it's the little faults and sins that, allowed to grow, expose not only the individual to danger but the whole family through their influence.

Monday morning at six o'clock, a number of people in addition to our family members, having heard in one way or another of our situation, came up to help with protecting our property. Marty Hirschkorn, David Sample, Jack Janetski, Brent Blaney, Paul and Jack Rayne, Mark Fink, Forest and Corla Rankin, Sam Jenkins, Aaron Jones, Kerry Garner, Tom Glatts, Dosung Kim, Paul Williams, Jerry Wernick, Rudy and Barbara Hall—all of you should know we will forever have a warm spot in our hearts for you dear people who came to help us. We dragged a massive pile of cut fuels away from the property and cleared the forest floor of debris, leaving a defendable space about the house, outbuildings, and property. Later that morning, I met a hand crew of twenty firefighters, who were unable to attack the fire directly due to the extreme danger. While talking with the crew leader, I asked if they would help us expand our work, and they agreed, happy to be able to do anything constructive against the fire, which had blown up in high winds late Sunday, expanding to more than 4,000 acres. I learned later that 2,000 of those acres burned in only twenty minutes! It was a sobering lesson on exactly what we faced.

It was all I could do to direct my work crews, but the devil is never satisfied simply to have our back up against the wall. He arranges circumstances so that just when we feel our cup is full and another problem would be impossible to handle, then he delights to drop at least one more problem upon us, which is exactly what happened to me that day! The starter on our large generator, our only source of power, died! Amid all this work to prepare the property, I had to tend to the repair as well.

I had told my helpers that we had until afternoon unhindered. In the afternoon, the winds would pick up, and then the fire would really start to move. It had been covering about two miles a day and was now less than three miles from our home—close enough that one could begin to feel the faint blush of heat from the distant conflagration. Rudy and Barbara took the starter to town for repair and were back with it by afternoon, but the generator still wouldn't operate properly. Jack searched out the problems carefully and had it working better by late afternoon. We gathered in the garage to eat a lovely lunch prepared by our friend Corla and enjoyed the fellowship of these dear friends and shared prayers for God's protection and strength. We were mentally prepared to fight the fire on into the evening, but afternoon brought an east wind instead of the expected west wind, and the fire was blown back on itself. It was almost as if God had said, *"Not yet. Jim and Sally need a little longer."*

God never brings temptations stronger than we can meet, and with the temptation He provides a way of escape. We often speak of God's grace as the favor He bestows upon us even though as failing sinful human beings, we are not deserving of such favor. I want you to understand that grace is far more than a generic kindness that God grants to every person. Grace is individualized for your personal need, and in this situation God knew and understood that for the last two days we had been pushed and pressured to prepare the property. He knew our personalities and our mental capacity, so in His mercy and love for us, He held back the fire to let us rest and regain strength for what was coming. He gave us *time* to prepare mentally and spiritually for the worst—whatever that might be.

To human reasoning, in spite of all the efforts put forth to prepare, our property was probably lost. The sheriff came by and informed us of the danger and that evacuation was ordered. However, Montana law does not require one to evacuate unless one is interfering with the firefighting. Both Sally and I felt in our hearts that God was not asking us to leave just yet. It was not that we were willing to trade our lives for the property, for certainly we were not. It was rather a studied conviction that we were not yet in danger, as we perceived it.

Everyone has his own comfort level when it comes to confronting danger. We like high adventure, and the recreation we engage in tends to have an edge of danger. We scuba dive with sharks; we jump out of airplanes and sky dive; we climb tall mountains and explore the wilderness. I have hiked as many of Glacier National Park's backcountry areas as almost anyone just because I like to be alone in nature with God. Grizzlies have charged me on occasion, and while the thrill of adventure is invigorating, even fraught with real danger at times, we are not adrenaline junkies seeking a fix. Our confidence is in God and His direction, not human wisdom, no matter how well reasoned.

The sheriff was the first of a number of officials who tried, over the next few days, to encourage, reason, even manipulate us into leaving. We explained our position, and they shook their heads sadly and theatrically requested information on how to contact our next of kin. We didn't respond to this well-intentioned manipulation, but knowing they were just doing their job, we simply signed the waiver stating that we chose to stay, recognizing our danger. You see, we had placed our confidence in God's leadership, a confidence we realized would have been impossible for us to exercise had we not been learning to let God lead for all these many years in the wilderness.

Because we chose to stay, we had a sign made that stood at the end of our driveway on the North Fork Road, so officials would know if we were on the property or gone. Back in the days when I sold real estate, I had a large log-framed business sign at the end of our driveway, which I have never removed, although now all real estate inquires are referred to my sons. A large piece of cardboard we hung over that old sign simply read, "Still Here." We didn't know it at the time, but this sign would become an icon reproduced on TV, in newspapers, even on the official government Web site for the fire.

After a good night's sleep we continued cleaning up the property, but the winds had shifted once again and were coming from the southwest. The fire started to run north toward Trail Creek. Fire crews began visiting our home, assessing our property and needs. With each crew, different suggestions were made and implemented. I can't say that the prospect of losing our home didn't stir up emotions and concerns in us, because it did, but both Sally and I worked through these feelings with God and accepted the idea of losing our home, property, and possessions if it was God's will. We were at peace and felt God assuring us that all was in His hands and would be well. The hard thing for us was that while we had this assurance, we didn't know if that meant He would be with us in our loss or prevent such a loss.

Representatives from a local TV station stopped in and talked with us. They liked our story and filmed while we explained why we were there when almost everyone else was gone. We gave the glory to God for the peace and lack of fear that we had experienced so far. We felt it was better to be there and do what we could to keep our place safe from spot fires than to leave and always wonder if our place was still there. The potential of losing everything was still vividly present. We would protect what we could, but we would not risk our lives for our home. Flesh is more valuable than logs, so we strove for that balance. This interview was shown during the ten o'clock local news that evening.

Dosung Kim brought an enclosed trailer with him to Monday's work bee, and he left it there for our use. Gradually we filled it with things that cannot be replaced—the important papers, pictures of the family, and other such items. Ed and Linda came over to visit in the afternoon. While the ladies visited, Ed and I climbed up to a knoll west of our property so we could see the direction of the fire's advance and judge its behavior. Sally and Linda had a very excited visitor during our absence. In her concern for our safety, the woman told Sally, "You've got to evacuate! The fire is going to cross the North Fork Road at Whale Creek just to the south of you, and the fire is also pushing across the North Fork Road to the north. If you don't leave *right now*, you'll be trapped with no way out!"

"Thank you," Sally told her, unconcerned. There were many false stories going around, spread by such well-meaning "Miss Informations." The smoke clouds to our west did not square with this story of rapid southbound expansion. We found out in the course of the fire that even information dispensed from official sources sometimes proved to be false. Yet how many of us respond to another's alarm without checking out the signs for ourselves? Many a person gathers a following by proclaiming the end is near only to leave their followers in doubt and despair when their predictions are shown to be fanciful imaginings of a mind not under the control of the Spirit of God. Other little Mr. and Miss Informations share supposed truths about friends, pastors, ministers, ministries—even whole churches and denominations fall victim to tales told by such well-meaning busybodies, who think nothing of destroying reputation and character to gain influence and power or to settle personal scores when offended. They are some of Satan's most effective agents; they have told his lies for so long that they sincerely believe the thing they share about others to be the truth. They think they are acting in love to protect you from someone else's errors. They work to destroy those who do not see things their way while assuring their victims of their love toward them. We need to be independent thinkers and remember that not every exciting piece of information that comes our way is true. This is why each must have their own connection to God and never rely on any other person to tell them what is truth and what is error.

Shortly after this a firefighter came to evacuate us, telling us a similar story. In spite of evidence to the contrary, Sally began packing our essential clothes and the last of the pictures as quickly as possible. Linda helped pack as sirens blew again and again, telling us it was the last call to evacuate, to drop everything and *run!* Ed and I had no idea what was happening at the house as we watched the fire from the knoll. Both women had called for us, but we couldn't hear them. We didn't even hear the sirens. We were just too far away. I listened to the story Sally told us when we returned, but I just couldn't believe it. I had just *been* on the ridge top and saw no immediate danger.

"Ed, I am not going to panic over other people's panic. You and Linda feel free to leave. We are going to finish packing up and then we will drive down and see if there is any truth to these rumors."

I could tell by his expression that Ed didn't like it, and I knew it was his love for us that motivated his displeasure, but he also knew I wasn't going to change my mind and at least I was going to *check out* the danger. So he and his wife drove away, while Sally and I returned to finish our work. I should, perhaps, take a minute and explain that we understood the danger of the situation, but we also know this area like other people know their backyards. We still had a number of escape options even if the road was closed, one of them being that we would run to the river and head downstream. We hurriedly packed up and drove down to the Whale Creek Road area only to find that the fire had indeed crossed Whale

Creek Road, but some five or six miles west of us. There wasn't any immediate danger to us at that point, so we returned home for the night and slept peacefully.

The next day was Thursday, six days after the fire was reported. To the west, the fire had crept to within about two miles of our home, but that evening the winds picked up and the northern extension to the fire took a mad dash eastward. By the time it reached the North Fork Road, it had formed a front almost three miles wide, the southern flank of which was only four-tenths of a mile north of us. We went to the east side of the North Fork Road, to an area along the river with an old airfield that happens to be one of our favorite places to walk. It is grizzly country, and we often see bear signs, even if we don't always see bears, but that evening all had changed. Sally and I watched what must be one of the most awe-inspiring sights a human being can ever witness. It showed all the fury of nature in a sin-scarred world. The fire swept in with 200-foot-high flames, and we watched as great trees would singe slightly, begin to smoke, and then with a roar and a pop explode into a pillar of flame. Moments later a nearby tree would repeat the process, and thus the fire steadily advanced. Neither the road nor the airstrip, not even the river slowed it down! It easily jumped the river and began burning its way into Glacier National Park.

At last, leaving nature's destructive display, we went to bed about ten-thirty. It's no surprise that we couldn't sleep. Rising about an hour later, we found the wind had shifted again and was now blowing from the north. The red glow we had witnessed to the north when we went to bed was now a red fireball. It was time to evacuate with our packed trailer, for we could lose it all tonight. We drove the miles south to Rudy and Barbara Hall's but just couldn't stay. Our longing hearts and our prayers were back in a little log cabin on the North Fork. So we dropped off the trailer and drove back to see if our place was still there. We arrived to find our prayers had been answered. The winds had died down and we were safe—for the moment, that is!

We went back to the Halls' place and slept well, if not long. It was impossible to open a window in the extremely smoky conditions. Driving north in the early morning to check the fire, we saw scenes of devastation, with spot fires everywhere. Around noon, the sky to our west turned brown and ugly; the smoke blew directly over our home. The fire to our west was now less than a mile away, and the northern flank only four-tenths of a mile distant. By anyone's standards, our property was endangered. The firefighter came once more and encouraged us to leave, but we just didn't feel the time had come.

Forest fire fighting has become more technical than many of us realize. Water has been the most commonly used substance to fight fires, and yet modern techniques have created ways to get more use out of every gallon of water expended. Wetting agents are added to the water, which decrease surface tension and allow smaller droplet formation and better sheeting and coverage. Certainly the Wedge Canyon fire provided us, if nothing else, an education in firefighting techniques. These firefighters had at their disposal knowledge gained over generations of firefighting—knowledge gained through much trial and error and sometimes at great personal sacrifice and suffering. As I watched them wet down all our buildings and then foam them, I couldn't help thinking of the parallels to the Christian walk.

These men didn't try and reinvent the rules for firefighting. They knew there was no substitute for hard work and understanding the formulas that brought success or failure to other people's efforts. For example, they knew that the fire needed fuel, oxygen, and heat to survive, and if they could break any part of this triangle, the fire would die and our buildings would survive. We had removed all the fuel we could except for our valuable trees and the buildings them-selves, and now they worked to wet and cool everything down, re-ducing the odds of super-heated materials combusting.

I thought of all the families I had met through my ministry who somehow thought that the rules that bring success in the Christian life didn't apply to them. They didn't think they needed to lower their risks, and for a time it seemed to work, but sooner or later the fires come to all of us. It may not be a literal fire, but the fires of passion, of greed, of stubborn pride, and human wisdom can lay waste to your home as readily as the worst forest fire.

The foaming of our structures was another lesson. The foam-ing agents transformed one hundred gallons of water into ten times as much—a thousand gallons of foam! This foam sealed in the moisture of the wet-down. It also sealed off small crevasses and nooks where an ember might find a little home in which to cause mischief. It reflected heat and cut off oxygen. It had fantastic wet-ting qualities and was basically easy to use. The simple combina-tion of water and the agent made the water into a much more effective tool for our salvation.

In exactly the same way, our human effort is like plain old water. Water poured on a fire has some effect, and human effort put forth to transform the life will also have an effect. This is why human good works become a substitute in many people's lives for a vibrant connection with the divine agent. However, if we were to step back and let God take control, putting forth effort at His direction and not our own, then we too would find our efforts, mixed with His, become ten times more effective than before.

The fire was closing in, and the firefighters placed a Mark 3 Wajax pump in our creek, utilizing the old cistern that had once supplied our home with water. I must admit I was fascinated with the thing. It's only twenty-two inches by twelve inches by sixteen inches and weighs slightly less than sixteen pounds, but I saw for myself why this pump is the standard wildfire pump in North America and in much of the world. The pressure and power of the stream this "little" pump could put out through a one-and-a-half-inch hose were extremely impressive. I found out later that it has a maximum flow rate of ninety-two gallons per minute and can provide up to 275 pounds of pressure per square inch. In our yard, two large-volume sprinklers were set up. One sprayed the west side of the garage and the other the west face of our cabin.

The firefighters would stay and conduct structure protection as long as they had an exit route. Around four o'clock, just as the fire started to move off the rise to the west and down toward us, suddenly the smoke ceased and in place of the angry brown smoke of moments before, only calm white puffs rose. The wind still blew the same as before, yet the silence was so complete and the change in the fire's behavior so marked that everyone seemed to sense something supernatural was afoot. Radio conversations died as we all watched the sudden change. In this island of calm, we stood still, watching and waiting as firefighters commented on the strange peace that had settled around us. The fire to our west had stopped as if a divine voice had said, "This far and no farther."

Meanwhile, to our south the fire was extremely active. The radios crackled to life with the news that the fire was moving off the bench south of us and was endangering the escape route. The radio voice ordered the fire crew to leave within sixty seconds. At first we didn't know what was going on as the firefighters rushed to leave, but as we caught on to the danger, we trusted the official information and left with them. We traveled south a short way to a meadow, where we stopped to watch what would happen.

This southern finger of the fire was coming at us like a roaring lion when suddenly the flames stopped and the fire settled down. After thirty minutes, we went back home to check on things. All was well, except that the pump had quit working. We restarted it and returned to watch from the meadow, but the fire never stirred. We decided to go back home for the night, once more awed by God's intervention on our behalf. The fire had never come down the ridge to our home, and we knew beyond a shadow of a doubt we had been kept in the cleft of His hand.

The next day, my son Matthew and I went up the back hill to check things out and found three spot fires. He fought the fires, and I hauled the water. It was a real team effort, reminding me once again how God takes care of those things we are incapable of handling, like the main forest fire, but He expects our cooperation in extinguishing those things within our control. Many small items like those spot fires are trying to do their devouring work in our lives, and like Matthew and I did, you may have to put forth some real effort to put them out. It was a hard lesson to miss as we hauled water up the hill in five-gallon buckets. Once the fires were out, Matthew left for home content in the knowledge that Andrew and Sarah planned to come up the next day.

The next afternoon, Andrew and I checked for spot fires, and we started finding them due west and others northwest. Andrew gamely started on the extinguishing, but I felt the need to get the big picture, so I said, "Andrew, I'm going to check out the rest of the situation. I'll be back as soon as possible." When I checked farther north, I gasped. Returning to Andrew, I told him, "There must be hundreds of spot fires running all the way north to the fire. This is way beyond our ability to handle. I'd better call incident command for reinforcements." The command center responded and put in a fire line along the base of the bench all the way from the area west of us to the fire perimeter to the north. We were mighty glad to see the skidder exposing dirt for the fire line, while a hand crew of about sixty firefighters worked areas the skidder couldn't go. However, the fire break was good protection from those creeping fires, but it would not stop the wind-driven monster we had glimpsed earlier, and this firebreak was now only 200 yards from our property, with the dragon lurking little more than a mile away.

Janell arrived, and no one could have been more welcome. She is not our daughter by birth but is certainly a part of our family. She has spent many hours in our home and has often ministered to our needs. She had originally planned to help us through a week of open house activities, but the fire had changed that. Still she came, and we were glad to have her.

After Matthew's wedding the previous summer, we had invited a number of people who wanted to come up and see our place to do so, and they came and really enjoyed their time at our home. We were astonished at how people knew the stories we have told in our sermons and books almost better than we did, and now they wanted to see the very spots where the stories took place for themselves. It was great fun to show them where the mother grizzly had sent her cubs up the tree and other tantalizing tidbits. Sally's mini open house was a smashing success, and this year we had decided to do it again and invite anyone who wanted to come. Janell had come to take over the running of our household to free us to visit with the people. We so wanted people to have a chance to enjoy the peace and quiet of the North Fork, to taste of our lifestyle in this special place and to be motivated to find their own special places, but now those plans were charred ruins. The open house had to be canceled, and while a few people would still drive or fly in, given the emergency situation, they would not be allowed past the roadblock.

It might seem a little odd, but when you work in a ministry where you see lives change and characters transformed before your very eyes, it's not hard for us to see this fire as Satan's attack to stop our open house, where many might have been helped to find a closer walk with God. Still, even amid the flame and smoke, God was active; for He is ever seeking after all, hoping they will respond.

Janell had not been with us long when she spied a spot fire and alerted us. While the firefighters were coming, together Janell and Sally brought section after section of garden hose to bear until our little hose reached the site of the fire. It was here that we met Mike, the division commander in charge of structures. He was going to be taking over command in our area.

Mike had a big heart, and when he saw the girls fighting the fire so valiantly with their tiny garden hoses, he asked, "You want me to get a fire truck in here for that?" However, the hand fire crew with shovels had lessened the flames, and the water from the girls' hoses put it out—dead! Still, he was concerned about ladies in the fire zone. Mike clearly would have preferred that we evacuate where we would be "safe." We explained our reasons for staying and could tell he wasn't too impressed with our ideas of "God's protection." However, he quickly realized we weren't going anywhere, and he would just have to keep our safety in mind while running this fire.

It was about this time that Sally met a woman working the fires. They had some heart-to-heart talks, and she shared with Sally that she just didn't know why circumstances had arranged for her to be fighting fires in the Montana wilderness that summer. Sally gave her a copy of our book, *Escape to God,* and later she told us, "I've been reading your book, and in it I've found out the reason why God has me up here this summer."

Things were getting very dangerous, and we now had a fire crew patrolling the property around the clock. The next day seemed critical, and Mike moved in a team of Hot Shots, the number-one fire team available. Neil and Billy White led this group, and in my opinion they definitely deserve the rank of number one! They have heart and soul, and they know how to work a fire. We watched in admiration one day as a fire flared in a section not far away from our home. Instead of running, this team rushed the flames with one fire hose, chain saws, and other equipment.

"Let's go, men. Let's go get it! Hustle—hustle—hustle!" I heard Billy White encouraging his gang, and go get it they did! The whole crew ran toward the fire. Chain saws screamed! Flaming trees crashed to the ground, each one felled perfectly back into the fire, away from us. Like battlefield commanders, Neil and Billy used all the resources available to them. Fire trucks arrived, followed by water trucks. All supported the fire team's efforts. All day they fought to protect our property with three fire trucks, a water truck, and the trusty Mark 3 pump in the creek.

At the time we didn't understand into what a quandary we put the fire bosses by our refusal to leave. First, no one likes someone looking over their shoulder as they do their job. Second, and the more complex issue for them, was that if we were hurt or killed, no matter how much we had been warned, it would bring them lots of negative publicity. Like all governmental agencies, the firefighters depend upon good publicity to generate a positive image in the public's eye to keep their funding. By and large, wildfire fighters are dedicated public servants who perform a vital service at great risk and for relatively little pay and thanks. Worse yet, they are often caught between conflicting policies and conflicting demands from the public they serve.

This is exactly what happened to Mike. Another landowner complained about the amount of protection we were receiving. His property was not as endangered, but the complaint prompted Mike to reassign two of the three fire engines as well as the water tender. The lack of the water tender meant that our fire truck had to leave our place and get its own tanks refilled.

So when we had only one fire truck, it headed off to refill. We were left with the Hot Shot crew, who, though very skilled, are still just a hand crew. They had no engines with multiple hoses and fast mobility to support their efforts or for retreat if it was needed in last-ditch structure protection.

The crew was working west to southwest of us when I heard the pump quit. *Oh, no,* I thought, and headed down to the creek to get it restarted. In the meantime, the crew came running out of the woods with shocking news! "The fire's coming down the bench with one hundred-foot flames! It's out of control! There's nothing more we can do. We're leaving!" they shouted as they ran. Sally was moving her water hoses when one tree, then two, exploded into flame just south of the guest cabin on the edge of the drive-way! "Jim, let's go," she shouted, and one glance at the fire told me she was right! Already flames were beginning to arch over the drive-way. As we prepared to head out, Mike returned. The paint on his truck was near the scorching point from the heat of the flaming tunnel through which he had just passed and through which we must now run in order to escape.

"Where are my fire engines?" I demanded.

"They're right behind me. You leaving?"

"Yes."

He hesitated for just a moment, and I found out later he al-most told us it was too dangerous to leave, but instead he said, "OK, we will be doing structure protection."

Less than five minutes had elapsed after that first warning of danger, but now trees were torching on *both* sides of the driveway. We drove through an archway of flames, praying that God's will be done—whatever that might be. The heat was intense, and with this benediction, all of us wondered if we'd see our home again. In an open field about a half mile south we watched the flames and the efforts against them as smoke rose in angry clouds above our place and advanced on the North Fork Road. The Hot Shots team found us and was as sad about the possible loss of our home as if it had been their own. "We did all we could," they sighed, but we brushed their apologies aside, trying to comfort and reassure them as much as possible. Truly there was nothing they or any human being could have done. It was all in God's hands now.

Helicopters clattered in overhead to drop their loads of water again and again. As near as we could judge from this distance, the drops were either on our place or very close to it. Additional fire trucks came up the North Fork Road. Even heavy equipment lumbered in. Watching all these valiant efforts, I gave voice to my thoughts at last. All day we had been protected with many, many firefighters, multiple fire trucks and water tenders, but all had been taken away. Even the pump had quit so that when the crisis came, there were no human defenders. "When we needed them most," I said, "no one was there."

"God can save by many or by few," Janell reminded me.

"You're right," I agreed. "I don't mind the loss of all that we have if it is God's will. What bothers me is standing here not knowing. I just don't like the not knowing what's happened."

At last, after almost three hours, I could stand it no longer. "I am going back to see what happened," I announced. "You girls can wait here if you want."

"Are you kidding? We wouldn't miss this for anything!" they replied, and off we went. What valiant ladies!

We were prepared for the worst, and what we saw on the way didn't encourage us. The firefighters had used the North Fork Road as a fire break. We passed a series of fire trucks all battling to keep the fire on the west side of the road.

Our driveway was full of thick smoke, yet a thin border of unburned trees lined the drive. Just beyond them we could see total devastation as far back as we could see. Almost everything in the fire's pathway south of our driveway was burned to a crisp. The driveway is not fully our property, but an easement through someone else's property. When we got to where we had escaped through flaming trees, we counted less than a dozen blackened trees. It didn't burn any farther. This didn't make sense. The fire should have burned to the edge of the drive, at least, and yet somehow the fire stopped, leaving us a small green barrier to shield us from the unending view of destruction. In spite of the wind, the main body of the fire had simply died down and advanced no farther, although a handful of spot fires had leaped over our property. They were the cause of the helicopter activity we had observed from the meadow.

All through the crisis, I had told everyone that I was more concerned with the loss of my mature trees than the potential loss of our home. I could rebuild our home in short order, but I could not do the same with the trees.

Strangely, though we had prayed that God might spare our property if it was His will, His restraint of the fire demonstrated to me just how personal His concern for me is. I don't know why, when we pray for a miracle and it happens, that we are so surprised, and yet we were. The guest cabin came into view and it was fine, surrounded by nothing but green. A D-6 caterpillar was making a dirt road as a fire break on the west side of the bench over on forest service land in line with our guest cabin. Little spot fires were burning all over the place west of that, and now and then a tree would flame up. The cabin, garage, and greenhouse all were intact, as were all our trees. Our house sat in the middle of a sea of green. Amazingly, God preserved not only our buildings but also our oasis of beautiful green trees!

Tears ran down my cheeks, for I had known that our home was not likely to survive, at least not as we knew it. We had visited another home that had survived the fire earlier, and while the foam and the firefighters had managed to save the structure, the fire had burned right up to the foundation, leaving an intact home surrounded by a desolate blackened landscape.

"Where have you been?" Mike shouted when he saw us.

I couldn't resist teasing him slightly, as waves of relief washed over me, "You've been trying to get me to leave for days!" Then turning serious, I inquired, "Mike, what happened?"

He looked at me as if to say, "You've been telling me about this God of yours that works for you and protects you, and you don't know what happened?" Mike stood there amid a sea of activity and said, "Jim, this has almost converted me. I have been thirty years in this work, and this was definitely divine intervention. Your God works for you in mysterious ways, and you are asking me what happened?"

Looking at our property filled with fire trucks and water trucks as well as scores of firefighters putting out the blazes, Mike told us the story of how he and his men had watched the fire come in and suddenly stop, as if an unseen hand held it back. The fire reared up under restraint, and the wind hurled flaming material past our property to start spot fires beyond us, but throughout this assault not a hose was raised in direct defense of our home. He stood on our porch and directed helicopters to drop their loads on the spot fires. He finally ordered his engines to put out the fire along the driveway, because clearly the house was safe for the moment, protected by more than human hands.

We joined the fire crews guarding the property from the remainder of the fire as countless hot embers scattered here and there. An atmosphere of celebration and camaraderie filled the air. Over and over firefighters congratulated us on the survival of our property and home. Everyone sensed that something special and unusual had happened here, and there was a certain joy in being on the winning side of a battle in a war which the firefighters had been waging without many victories. Our home was a victory won by God, and we all realized we were just mopping up.

The next day Mike drove in and asked us how we were doing. Matthew and Angela, as well as Andrew and Sarah, had come up and camped out on the living-room floor. In the tightly closed cabin, the heat was oppressive, but the smoke was too thick to even think about opening a window. "We slept great," I told Mike.

"I hear down the valley that you're an author."

"That's right."

"I'd like to read your book."

So I went and got Mike an *Escape to God* copy and wrote in the front:

Dear Mike,

God wants to work for you in mysterious ways too,

God bless,

Jim

And dear friend, God wants to work for you too . . . in mysterious ways. The question is always, "Will you let Him?"

Throughout this book I have shared the positive aspects of coming to the quiet. I make no apologies for it because modern life increasingly brings cares and concerns to us that have no reason or right to add to the stresses of life we carry. We are bombarded with news of disasters, unspeakable crime, and chaos in the investment industry. These bad-news stories tend to guide our thinking into a state of crisis that builds tension and the fear of some mysterious something that might happen to us.

A friend told me that a group of workers in his company was talking one day about how bad the economy was. My friend was taken aback, for most of those talking had secure jobs and were earning six figures or close to it, so he inquired if things were going bad for them personally.

"Oh, no, it's just that so many people are out of work," they responded.

"Do you know someone personally who has lost their job?" he pressed. Not one did. They were stressed out about things that didn't affect them directly or even indirectly through friends or acquaintances. Our forefathers would never have been troubled by such reports. They lived in the quiet of God's great out-of-doors. They worked hard and played hard. When they went to bed, it was with the wholesome fatigue of exercise rather than the never-ending stress of mental concern and the continuous and steady diet of excitement that causes restlessness and dissatisfaction.

Coming to God's quiet places us in a situation where we are, to a large degree, sheltered from the artificial strain Satan so often uses to bind modern man. Here amid the quiet and grandeur of God's creation, we are better able to judge the true from the false. The devil knows if we continue in this pathway for long, his hold upon us will be continually weakened, and he is aroused to bring trial and trouble upon us. In this story of our fire, I want you to see as never before that the wrath of our enemy will be poured out upon any who try and live God's way. There is no guarantee of pleasant conditions or a trouble-free life.

Every one of us is going to face the fire of destruction in some way or another, and the only way we survive is by having a living connection to the God of heaven. I wish there was some way I could demonstrate adequately the security that comes from full surrender and commitment to God. There is an old-country saying that has it about right: "It's in you what ails you." External trouble, like the fire, could not rob us of our peace and the security of heaven's watch-care over us. Only when we have something inside that is not surrendered and dealt with, only when there is a cherished area left untouched by God, can the enemy of our souls find an answering chord in our hearts to magnify his temptations and drag us into uncertainty. Don't wait until the fire comes to try and gain the connection you need with God. It may be too late when the crisis comes. Today is the day, and now is the hour to come to the quiet of God's presence. Heaven will never be nearer than it is today.

Huge flames near driveway

Fire crew approaching

The sign at the end of the driveway

Fire engine by the log cabin

Mop-up crew

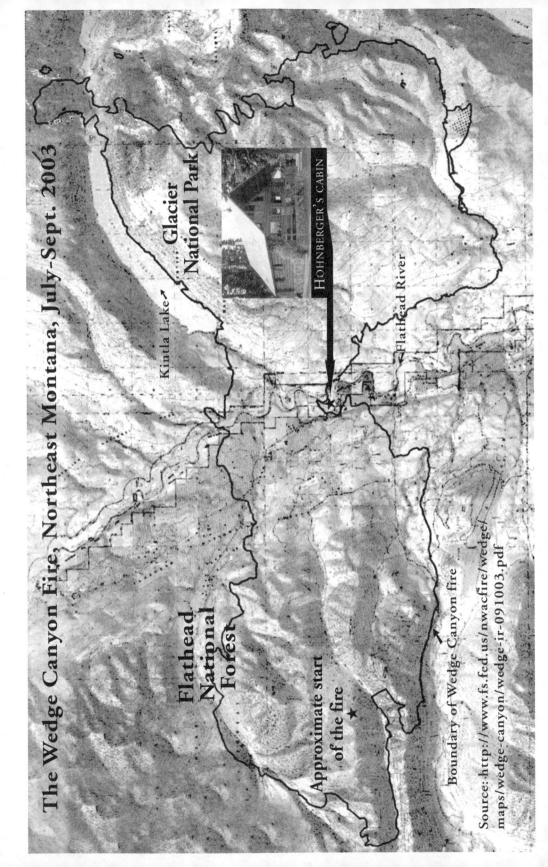

The Wedge Canyon Fire, Northeast Montana, July–Sept. 2003

Glacier National Park

Kintla Lake →

HOHNBERGER'S CABIN

Flathead River

Flathead National Forest

Approximate start of the fire ★

Boundary of Wedge Canyon fire

Source: http://www.fs.fed.us/nwacfire/wedge/maps/wedge-canyon/wedge-ir-091003.pdf

CHAPTER 13

EMBERS

And of some have compassion, making a difference: And others save with fear, pulling them out of the fire; hating even the garment spotted by the flesh (Jude 22, 23).

The next day dawned warm and smoky, but Matthew and his wife Angela, Andrew and his wife Sarah, Sally and I, and even Janell were up early and walking about, looking for the numerous spot fires that burned here and there. We went about the job, enthusiastically praising God that we still had a property to defend and for the miracles He had performed. We did our job so well that when the fire crews arrived, they congratulated us for us for making their task easier. Yesterday had been a turning point in our relationship with them. We were no longer just stubborn homeowners refusing to leave but now accepted as part of one team working to save the property.

Mike, the division commander, brought in a large crew to mop up everything. He was very tenderhearted and kind toward us. The feeling that we had survived was very pervasive, but Mike pointed out, "You are still in extreme danger for at least another week." I could tell he hated to give us this bad news, and Sally explained that while we listened carefully to what others told us, in the end we filtered it all through God, and He would continue to direct and protect us.

The desperate run the fire had made at our property the day before seemed to change the whole attitude about the property and us. Earlier, the firefighters had been kind, concerned, and as professional as could be. Now there was a new sentiment in the air. Everyone had seen our property spared when it seemed impossible, and it was as if they all viewed our home as some special place. It was reflected in their continual care and concern.

Our place soon became a hub of activity, and for the next few days it was like Grand Central Station. Under the circumstances, we were very grateful. Mike even held his divisional command meetings on our lawn, giving us frequent contact with him, and more important, his knowledge about firefighting plans. One day he finished his meeting and wandered over to us to exchange greetings.

"Mike, will it be quiet today?" Sally asked.

"No, the weather service has marked it as a red-flag day for high winds and prime fire conditions. We are very nervous about the other two ends of this fire, the Trail Creek and Moose Creek areas. I'll be pulling all my equipment and dividing it between these two areas because we are expecting the worst. I'll leave you the Hot Shots for the moment. You should be safe with them. The forecast is high winds and more lightning without rain," Mike answered, as he glanced skyward, his face gravely serious.

"We will make it a point to pray to God to eliminate the high winds and ask for no lightning," we reassured him.

"I appreciate it. This is awful, and we are all so tired. My crews are exhausted. Well, we've got to get moving. You know how to call us if you need us."

God answered our prayers, and we had no lightning or high winds that day. Praise God! Mike was pleased for a little reprieve to let his crews rest and catch up, and we were delighted that God demonstrated yet again the power of prayer.

Another day I witnessed a more humorous incident. It is not easy for a commander like Mike to find even a single quiet moment to himself, and one day I watched as he drove in and climbed wearily out of the truck with his lunch. It was hot, and he spied a shady spot under a tree amid the beautiful green of Sally's lawn. Before I could even get outside to utter a word of warning, he flopped tiredly to the ground, but not for long! I had gotten to the door just in time to see him leap up, and I heard him mutter, "That Sally! She's been watering again!" He turned to head farther into the woods, his backside clearly wet. Poor Mike. I felt bad after all he'd done for us!

We were thankful for our Hot Shot crew (at least, that's how we thought of them), which was mopping up once more on our property. They had just put out another large spot fire when one of them called out, "Sally, Sally, come here. We have a bunny we just caught and saved from the fire! Will you take care of it?"

A helpless and injured little bunny—who could resist? She had one eye that was burned, leaving a cataractlike look. Her paws were extremely hot, and she was very frightened. All things considered, she was a very lucky hare.

"What shall we name her?" I asked Sally.

"I don't know. Let's have a contest and let the workers choose."

Days later, we settled on "Embers." She stayed inside with us for a week. While Sally doctored her injuries, it seemed the thing that helped her most was just eating and eating and eating. But don't think that Embers simply took from us, no indeed! Embers was a symbol of all that is good and kind, all that still remains in the heart of man from his Creator.

Embers became a kind of celebrity. Everyone wanted to see her, rub her fur, and check on her burns. Embers could easily interrupt the division meetings if Sally took her outside while Mike was talking. He and his staff always crowded around to see her. She was exactly what everyone was working for, a visible sign of success. She may have been only a half-grown hare, but she was about all that anyone was seeing rescued from this fire, and everyone loved her precisely because she reminded them of better times and a sweeter type of communing with nature than they currently enjoyed.

This is exactly what coming to the quiet is all about. It's catching a glimpse of a different and better way of life, more in touch with nature and nature's God. These firefighters had much to do, yet one of God's tiny creatures awakened in them love and tenderness for a helpless suffering one that was truly a reflection of the divine character. You may feel your loved one or your family is so far gone that there is no hope of things ever getting better, but I want to assure you that no one is so callous or so hardened that God cannot awaken in them the most tender of feelings. No matter how far we have wandered from truly reflecting God's character, He is working circumstances that we may be changed into His image. Things may look very bleak in our lives, but it is at the darkest hour when the flames threaten our destruction, that a salvation we could never have imagined has been prepared for us, and a divine hand is stretched forth to remove us from danger.

You and I are just like little Embers, caught and injured in a world seemingly aflame with sin. Yet in the midst of the world's terrible battle for survival, God's tender heart of sympathy is drawn out to us personally. He longs to take us in His hands, to bind up our wounds, and to feed us on the best of the land, just as we did with Embers.

Embers was in a place of danger, and the only way of safety for her was the way that frightened her even more—and that was captivity in human hands. She was scared to death and shook with fright. Yet to remain in a sea of fire was to court certain death. How many of us live where we will die spiritually and not even sense the danger? We often know deep within our souls that our heart's longings are not being met and that the hurts and wounds of life have not been healed. Many, many are members of the church, even leaders of the church, and yet if they were examined by the Great Physician, they would be classified as walking wounded, just like Embers.

Finding a cure will require that we move outside of our comfort zone. Embers had to surrender her will to ours for her own good, and so must we learn to surrender our will to God for the good of our family and our own souls. But how few are ever willing to take such a step? Embers was captive to us. For her own salvation, we had to decide where she could go and what she could do. This crossed her will and she didn't always like it, but she quickly adjusted and learned to thrive under our care. You and I have minds that need to be brought into captivity to Christ and hence the will of God. Giving God the control is a learning experience and one our self-will will not enjoy, but an experience that is vital to our salvation. Embers' home was a large Rubbermaid tote, and she wanted to get out in the worst way. In like manner, many of us see the restrictions of God as nothing more than a dull and imprisoning structure. Yet if we will learn to submit, He will feed us and care for us, and we, too, will thrive like Embers did.

The God of heaven is reaching out to you and me, trying to save us, but most of us run this way and that to escape capture. He is far too gentle to use force and possibly hurt us. When the time was right, we set Embers free to enjoy the clover and green grass of our North Fork home. If we are willing to submit to His guidance, God promises that He will care for us and will eventually free us in the pastures of the new world, where the fires of sin can never again harm us. Are you in His care today? You can be. He will draw all who do not resist. Yes, surrender to God is scary, but it is the only path to safety both in this world and in the kingdom to come.

CHAPTER 14

FRUSTRATION

I will never leave thee, nor forsake thee (Hebrews 13:5).

Our "Still Here" sign became something of an icon to the fire crews working the North Fork Road. Certainly we were one of the few families that had chosen to stick it out, and the story of our home's survival had spread far and wide. Every new crew came in knowing all about our home and had adopted the attitude that they were working to save a very special place, and they were right! We made a sign to add to our "Still Here" sign at the end of the driveway, which read, "Thanks to Fire Crews!" It was our way of expressing heartfelt thanks to these people who had done so much to assist God in the saving of our property.

Sadly, we lost "our" Hot Shots crew as mopping up continued. In truth, this was a good sign because we were no longer considered endangered enough to rate a Hot Shot crew, and two new crews were moved in to mop up, one to work our property westward and another to work from our property line northward. I didn't realize that this morning was the calm before one of the greatest personal challenges I have ever faced.

I am an efficient person, and I hate to see things done in a haphazard manner, which is perhaps why I liked the Hot Shot firefighters so well. Yet, from the time I moved to the wilderness I have faced this weak area of my life over and over in a way that I never faced it in the more hurried life back in Wisconsin. If something frustrated me there, I soon gave way to my flesh and let everyone know exactly how I felt about the situation. Now as I sought to become a true Christian, if my experience was anything to go by, God certainly wanted me to overcome this weakness because I frequently found my plans thwarted, my wishes denied, my ideas discounted, and even the simplest of tasks complicated beyond all reasonableness. I knew the Bible spoke of the patience of the saints, but I had no idea when I became a Christian that patience was a spiritual gift obtained through trial. Later, when I read that even Christ learned obedience through the things He suffered, I was strangely comforted. I don't like this type of learning, and yet God allows it for my benefit. In my two decades in the wilderness, I have come to understand to some degree that when such things happen they are designed to strengthen me and improve my dependence upon God.

Our two crews of firefighters were coming back off the line after hours of work. They had run hose from the pump in our creek some hundreds of feet back into the woods. Now in the late afternoon sun, a number of grubby, tired firefighters lay down in the inviting green grass of our lawn, while still others sat on the hillside overlooking the creek where the pump was. Clearly they were strung out, disorganized, and tired. This crew didn't work as hard as the Hot Shots, but not every crew is going to compare favorably with the number-one crew. Still I was a little uneasy to have our proven friends unavailable, and though this crew seemed nice enough, we missed the easygoing companionship and bond that we had developed with the Native American crew.

We were outside when a gust of wind caught our attention as it flowed in from the west. All eyes were drawn to the bench where the fire flared and immediately flowed down to the trees behind the guest cabin. The wind picked up and energized the fire, which roared toward the guest cabin.

"Fire! Fire!" We shouted to the crew chiefs, pointing in alarm at the latest outbreak, expecting the same type of decisive orders and action we had seen in the past weeks, but they did *nothing*. They just stood there. I couldn't believe it.

We waited, expecting some sort of action, but even the leaders did nothing! At first it just didn't register with me. I just stood there with my mouth open. *Surely they plan to do something,* I thought, but nothing happened. I glanced back at the spreading flames. If someone didn't act fast, this was going to get out of control.

"This is crazy! The firemen's lives are in danger too—why don't they do something?" Sally whispered in my ear.

"I don't know, but if they don't act, we'll have to!"

I turned to some firefighters and said, "Let's get the hoses out of the low lands and knock this fire down out of the trees." No one moved. They just stood there as if frozen. I don't know if you have flesh like mine, but I could just feel the frustration begin to rise within me. I wanted to make them take action, do something, anything to start them moving, but is that Christianity—to force my will on another? I realized I was beginning to give way to frustration and surrendered it to God, but that didn't remove my problem with these firefighters. I strove to find a solution before it was too late.

Maybe if I start working, they'll join me, I thought. Sometimes it just takes one person moving to prompt others to respond, so I went over to the hose and tried to pull it up the hill. I couldn't even budge it, and no one came to help. You must remember that moving those loaded fire hoses is like trying to wrestle a python, and when they're filled, they weigh hundreds of pounds. Talk about irritation. Here our home had survived the worst the fire could throw at it, only to be endangered because I had a crew that didn't seem to want to fight the fire.

"Please help me!" I pleaded, but they acted like the idea of moving the heavy hose from down the hill was way beyond the call of duty. I had to do something, and fast. The water-truck driver pulled up, and I asked Bill, the driver, to help me pull the hose, but he and I still couldn't do it. "Bill, have you worked with a crew like this? Do you know how to get them to help?" The fire crew was looking at me like I was some crazy homeowner who didn't belong in a fire zone. They didn't say a word, but their actions said, "Who do you think you are, trying to boss us around like this?" I could tell the fire was advancing rapidly and whatever moments that the situation had allowed for discussion were rapidly ticking away. Ten minutes or so was all the guest cabin had left if it was to be saved.

Bill began to "speak" to the crew using some rather colorful phrases, and it *did* get them moving. The hose started to come out of the low land, and, thinking they were going to get the hose over to the fire, I went down to start the almost-always stubborn pump, knowing this might take a few moments and every moment counted. I had no idea what was happening up above me by the house. When my head cleared the hillside after starting the pump, I couldn't believe what I saw. Part of one crew was working on the hoses, but it looked as if the Keystone Cops or the Three Stooges had come instead of firefighters. The hose sections had come apart, or maybe they had taken them apart for transport, but not knowing this, I had turned on the water, which was spraying out on everyone and everything—except the fire! The crew tried frantically to get sections back together as hose flailed this way and that, spraying all the while like a fountain gone wild.

Can you enter into this problem with me for a moment? I mean, how hard can it be to take a hose a few hundred feet through the cleared woods to defend the guest cabin? I wanted to tell these "guys" (actually a less complimentary term came up in my thoughts to describe them) what I thought of them right then and there. Wouldn't you? I am so thankful to God because along with these thoughts came His impression saying, *"Jim, is that going to put out the fire?"*

"No, Lord. You can have these feelings," I told God as I rushed back down the hill to shut down the pump. After what seemed an eternity, they got the hose close to the fire. I ran all the way back to the pump, past men standing around watching, past the men lying in the yard watching, past the guys sitting on the hillside watching, and with every one of them I felt the desire to tell them off, to give way to temptation, to stop being a Christian. I was never so grateful to have gone through so many trying circumstances in the past because those experiences enabled me to stay focused upon God and surrender the upset feelings that kept coming back.

I restarted the machine and pressurized the hose, and then I ran all the way back to the other end to man the hose because once more my professional firefighters were not doing their job! Realizing we needed more hose sections, I handed the nozzle off to Bill and headed back to get them. The frustrations I faced in this simple task must have been designed by the devil himself to press all of my hot buttons. Only later I realized that, like Job of old, God had placed a hedge of protection about me and my property. Satan knew he couldn't harm me as long as I remained faithful to God, so he decided to help his cause by so ordering events that he could apply pressure on my weakest point. It is the area of frustration and anger that he has tripped me up again and again over the years, and in this instance he was resorting to them again.

I am a person who looks for solutions. God has blessed me with quick vision, and I don't need to study a problem for long to know what needs to be done to solve it. I do not do well when others do foolish things, or when poor reasoning or blind adherence to rules leads to choices that follow no rational approach. People fighting forest fires have a problem. In the big, long-term picture, and by this I mean over hundreds of years, fires serve a useful purpose in the forest's life span. I do not disagree with this reasoning; it is just that I do not believe our old planet has hundreds of years left for us to worry about. Unfortunately, this reasoning about the benefit of fire has led many wildfire managers to adopt the "let it burn" policy, which means they will attack fires only when they enter private property.

I have no idea if this type of reasoning was at work, but it appeared so when I got back to the house to get more hose. The one crew had spread itself out along our property line as if all set to defend it. In a way I understood their action and their earlier inaction. After all, there were thousands of acres of forest burning all about us, almost all of it government land, so why was I getting worked up about an outbreak on forest service land? In the big-picture mind-set, this followed a certain mad logic, but in the meantime they were allowing this fire burning just off our property to grow into something no hand crew in the world could ever stop once it reached private property. It made no sense to me, and trying to reason with them at that point would make even less sense. The remains of the second crew still lay about the yard, and it really bothered me. By now it seemed I had been fighting this fire alone forever. I am in good physical condition, but I am not young anymore, and I was getting tired. The devil loves to get us tired. He knows we get weaker in our resolve if he can keep up the pressure and cause us to enter into a long, protracted battle with temptation.

I wasn't exactly diplomatic; however, I needed help and needed it badly. "Get off your butts and come help me get more hose sections," I called to them. A few reluctantly got up, and once more the frustration seemed to rise of its own free will as I saw others just sitting there as if daring me to make them move. Again I could sense God urging me to surrender it to Him, and I did. My voice softened under God's influence. "Come on," I encouraged. "We've got a major fire to deal with."

Bill came up, evidently having passed his hose on to someone else. He too had come looking for more hose, and when he saw the men still lying there, he used some rather sharp and uncomplimentary words with them. Evidently what he said was effective because one of the men got all puffed up and said, "You can't talk to me that way, I quit!" and with a little-boy pout, he stomped over to one of their vehicles. What an attitude! Here we are facing destruction, and he quits because he doesn't like the way someone talked to him. Outrageous, you say? Maybe so, but it is hardly unusual.

Today I find many in the church who are just like these firefighters. They just sit and watch as others prepare to fight the battles of the Lord. Others only act when prompted by those who see the danger, and then only partway. There are even those in the church who quit the moment someone speaks to them in a way they don't like. Many a man in the church stands by and lets his wife try to fight the battle to save the children from the world while his help is desperately needed. The weak one should not be leading out, yet he lies there watching those less qualified, but sincere, struggle just like those firefighters watched us.

It looked so impossible that any help would come from human sources that Janell and Sally knelt down right there in front of everyone and started pleading to God for help. The God of heaven is ever near to answer the prayer of faith, and the wind immediately died down. A fire truck came up the driveway, and the men onboard, seeing the situation, started spraying the fire from the south side. When Bill and I got back with the hose, things looked much better, and with the new hose sections added we were able to knock the fire down.

I still was shocked at the behavior we had seen, and when I noticed a supervisor among the fire-truck crew, I asked if he could reach Mike, the division commander, on the radio and ask him to come by because I needed to talk with him. Mike drove in after a while, and I spoke very carefully to him. I realized right from the start that I could be in real trouble, for while in Montana you cannot be forcibly evacuated, you can be removed if you interfere with firefighting, and I had just done far more than interfere. I had taken over command and exercised authority I didn't have. I was very concerned about the situation. In my heart I felt I had done what I had to do. However, I was not blind to the possibility that someone else might take my actions the wrong way and possibly be within their rights to ask the sheriff to remove me.

Before going into the whole story I apologized for exercising authority I didn't have the right to take, and then I laid out my whole tale. Mike listened and said, "You don't owe me an apology at all. You did what needed to be done. It is I who needs to apologize to you for what men under my command did." Mike was very apologetic about this situation. He ordered in fire trucks, water trucks, and manpower to begin watering and building a fire line to contain the outbreak. He could see that the fire had gotten perilously close to a huge one hundred-by-fifteen-foot-wide area of brush that had been cleared during the thinning of our property. This ten-foot-high pile could have ignited a disaster for us, and we all knew it. He couldn't seem to do enough for us to make up for what had happened.

"It's all right Mike, it's all right," Sally said. "God has taken care of us. We are all right now. It's all under control again. It's OK—really!"

As Mike evaluated the fire he called for helicopter drops of retardant and water on the fire to the north of us, which unknown to us during the crisis, had made another run on us, but the wind had changed to push it back. What a loving God we have, who watches over us even when we don't know the danger we are in.

In exactly this same way, God is ordering events in your life just now. Only in eternity will we have any idea of the loving care God invests in every one of us. Just because we see no danger does not mean He does not see or care, and God never allows Satan to bring upon us more trouble than we can bear; indeed, He often cares for much beyond our vision and ability. Every action of God is in loving concern for His children.

The next day we were planning a trip into Kalispell to meet with those families that had come to Montana despite the cancellation of the open house. But how could we go now? The idea of leaving our home after what had just happened seemed impossible, but Matthew and Angela offered to come up and keep an eye on things so we could go to Kalispell and meet the people.

Before we could leave for town the next morning, Mike came by and told us, "I don't want you to worry one bit about your property while you are gone. I will personally see to it that it's kept safe. I am going to bring in my whole division's resources to protect your place. That's 200 men, 23 fire trucks, and water tenders. I want you to understand what I have told them. They are to touch every tree, stick, and piece of ground for 300 yards in every direction of your property and if there is any warmth at all, it is to be soaked with water." He assured us that he would put out everything from north to south and everything on the west side as well before the day was over!

So we started down the driveway, and even though the hour was early, Mike was as good as his word. Buses had lined the North Fork Road, and 200 firefighters in their yellow Nomex shirts, bright spots in the smoky morning gloom, were marching down our drive-way, followed by fire truck after fire truck, and tankers after them. It was an astonishing display of firefighting might. There are some whole fires that don't get this much attention, and here were little old Jim and Sally Hohnberger resting in the care of the mighty army God had sent.

Truly God does work in mysterious ways! Everything good comes from God. We were grateful to Mike, but our supreme thanks go to God! This huge trial that frustrated me to no end when our firefighters would not help us was a tool used of God to bring in more help than we ever could have hoped to receive. The difficul-ties and trials God allows are often His greatest blessings to us if only we could see the Almighty's hand working circumstances for our benefit instead of the irksome problems that our trials often seem to be in our limited human wisdom.

Matthew and Angela were already on their way, and they brought a whole cooler full of frozen fruit. At our house, they made ice-cold smoothies for all the firefighters. Everyone had all they wanted. Firemen used their radios to invite all who'd like to come. Matthew just loved it. There were groups here and there "filling" our yard, but the uncooperative crew of the day before had not come up.

"This isn't right," Matthew said to himself. "God forgives us when we make a mistake, and we need to seek out these people, not let them stay excluded." So he went out and found the crew. They hemmed and hawed for a while, not feeling they deserved any reward, but as those who have had to negotiate with Mat-thew find out, he can be quite persuasive and made sure they got served as well. In truth, there were many good men on that team. They just lacked leadership. We appreciated all that they did as well. We are eternally grateful to all who helped God preserve our property.

We didn't know it at the time, but several firefighters told us about a speech that Mike, the division commander, had held back at the fire camp in front of the many hundreds of firefighters not just in his division, but the whole fire crew. Mike characteristically never said a word to us about it, and we will probably never know his exact words, just the reports of others. He was all choked up as he told our story of fighting the fire on our own without the help of the firefighters. "Wow, was he upset!" was the way one of the firemen reported it and then continued to quote Mike's words. "When we watch a family fighting the fire and do not come to their aid, we have lost the total essence of what it means to be a firefighter. This has happened once. It must never happen again."

If you could sit tonight in heaven's fire camp and listen as Christ talked about the events of the day, what would He say? What stories would He tell of your area of responsibility? Did you see the ones in trouble today, the ones just barely hanging in amid the fire of sin, of immorality, of worldly influences, and of discouragement? Or did you only see the children in your family as the same boys and girls you see everyday and never really see the struggle of their lives? Did you see that person you married as an individual in need or only as your spouse and take them and their love for granted? Every one of us has people depending upon us. Are we being faithful to that trust? If not, don't hide off in the woods feeling bad about your failure. Come forward, accept their forgiveness, and through the strength of Christ, determine that in the hour of danger you will never be found wanting again!

The fact that Satan was determined to destroy not only our family but our property should not come as a surprise to any of us. Our home was the place where we grew up in the Christian walk—our incubator if you will—and from this location has come not only the life-transforming message we share but a worldwide ministry, and countless tapes, books, and videos. The destruction of our property would have been a huge distraction from our work, although I do not doubt that God would have brought good out of the situation for us. In truth our enemy would have been delighted to distract us, even more he would have been delighted to have used the frustrations of his manipulated circumstances to get us to let go of God and depend fully upon our own strength. It is to learn how not to do that very thing that God leads us to country homes and quiet settings so He can teach us dependence upon Him and a distrustfulness of our own wisdom.

If you choose to follow my family in this pathway, you too will face fires. Oh, they may not be the fires of a wilderness forest, but they may be of the much more dangerous type kindled by critics, by mischief-makers, by those who, because of their own ambitions, see anyone presenting the powerful message of the gospel as a threat to their influence. Great men of every age have had to face such trials, and if you would follow in their steps, you must be prepared to do the same.

Coming to the quiet and learning to live in the quiet of God's presence amid life's most trying circumstances provides us with the ability to welcome life's joys even at stressful times. By coming to the quiet, I found myself at peace in the midst of this fire. I was able to form friendships with firefighters, able to enjoy my family and marvel at the special bond we have together. This is what God desires to provide you as well. May His richest blessings be yours because you chose to come to the quiet and remain there in His presence amid whatever struggles you face.

CHAPTER 15

REFLECTIONS

O give thanks unto the LORD; for he is good: for his mercy endureth for ever (Psalm 136:1).

The open house week ended, and I was led to think about what might have been. There was no question in my mind that the devil designed the fire to destroy us and our influence, but like so many of his plans, our enemy could not have known how God would use this fire for good. Rain fell that day—not much, but it quieted things down.

Embers was ready for release, and Sally let her go near the greenhouse, where the wood pile provided some hiding places. In truth, there was no brush left to hide in as it was all cleared. We hope Embers will continue to do well, but only time will tell. So far we have spotted her a few times, and she is in good shape and adapting well to her injuries.

The fire continued to burn across the river in parts to the east. We sat at the table, eating lunch, and the smoke really started pouring up. Sally and Janell commented that it looked as though it was coming at us. "No way!" I told them. "There's no way it's coming from the east."

Yet after lunch, when I went to look, it was! It was galloping toward the river and us. I drove down to a neighbor whose home is closer to the river than ours, and there I found the fire was indeed coming back at us from the east. My neighbor said the fire crews had already been notified. I couldn't believe it! The fire had already made several attempts at our home, and now it was going to try and come at us from the one unburned side in the east?

"Lord, rebuke Satan and his evil plans," I prayed. "Enough is enough!" Praise God! The fire closed on the river and then receded.

Now we faced a hard choice. We had planned to go to the Quetico, a wilderness canoe area in Canada, with Matthew and Angela. The extreme fire danger had passed, yet the possibility of a hot ember coming to life was always there and could cause us problems for many weeks to come. Could we still go on our trip, trusting God that our home would be safe? We decided we could go! The firefighters promised to check the house morning and night.

Once that was decided, we started preparing to leave. I had to go to town and see the dentist, and since we were going to be away for Andrew's birthday, we decided to get together that evening at his house and celebrate early. Janell had been looking forward to the birthday party, but the constant stress, smoke, and strain had taken its toll, and she had come down with a sore throat and cold symptoms. Disappointed, she decided she did not want to take the chance of passing it along to Matthew and Angela just before they headed into the canoe wilderness, so she opted to stay home.

As we drove off to town, I thought about Janell. She had come across the country to help us simply out of loving concern, and she had worked hard all week at our moment of maximum danger, and now she was sick. I just hated sin at that moment, and all the suffering it has caused. I prayed she would get well soon. In my human wisdom that was all I understood of the situation, yet God has promised that all things work together for good to them that love the Lord. How this could work for the good was beyond me.

We had a wonderful time with our family and left late for the long drive up the North Fork Road. By the time we got home, it was very late, and everything seemed peaceful. But after Janell's call in which she shared the story of her afternoon, we knew that was not the case.

About five o'clock Janell went out to move Sally's hoses to water a new section of lawn, and she saw a column of smoke drifting up behind the greenhouse. Taking the backpack water carrier that the firefighters had left for our use in just such situations, she headed into the woods to investigate. Less than 500 feet from the greenhouse, she found a large spot fire. Whether it had drifted in that day or had sat slowly burning from the previous week it was impossible to know, but that day it had sprung to life, and already it was way beyond anything she could hope to put out on her own.

Running back to the house, she quickly dialed the number of the incident command center and in an incredibly short ten minutes, two fire trucks arrived to handle the problem. If Janell had been well and had gone with us, this spot fire would have had at least five hours more to expand and grow. We could have lost everything. Surely all things do work for good!

The entire story of the fire is one endless tale of divine intervention. We have a horseshoe of burned land around our property. Yet our loving God left us with a green oasis. We only lost a half acre of trees that we could not see on our south side. Our views are nicely intact on all four sides of us. If we consider the area on the other side of the river that burned to our east, we have had the fire burn around us in nearly a circle while we have been repeatedly spared. Isaiah 43:2 says it so well. "When thou walkest through the fire, thou shalt not be burned; neither shall the flame kindle upon thee." God is good. He can bring good out of difficult, trying, and yes, even devastating situations.

There was another and even more dear divine intervention on our behalf during this fire. The same God who controls the elements kept us at peace throughout the fire. In a way, I guess this is fitting. We came to these mountains, to the quiet, because the fires kindled by our uncontrolled self-wills were consuming our love for each other and our family. Now some two decades later, we have once again been brought back to face the fires in our lives, and, oh, what a difference our relationship with the Lord had made this time around. We have learned how to have peace within the storm, blessed peace that allows us to sleep right through the storms of life.

In order to find this, we had to move to the quiet, to come to the quiet, and away from a decaying society and world so ready to suck us into its way of doing things so that we would become like every other dissatisfied couple. We praise God that this was not our fate. Today we are living the same dream we had so many years ago, drawing closer to each other and, together, closer to God. Not everyone is called to live the type of life we have, but every one of us is called to find the quiet that is found in the presence of God.

He is speaking to you today, asking if you have had enough of bearing your own burdens. He is standing before you and asking you to come unto Him and find the rest that your soul longs for. I, too, would add my poor voice to His, encouraging you to come; that's all you need to do. Come to God, and He will tell you your duty. It is my heart's desire that you, too, might taste of the quiet in your life. I believe it is your heart's desire as well. Will you grant it? Will you risk what it takes to obtain it? Will you come to the quiet?

The Hohnbergers' log home

Grizzly and cubs in front yard

Matthew and Andrew, aged 8 and 6

Andrew feeding a 10-point buck

Couch games with Dad

Embers, the rescued rabbit

Other best-selling books from Jim Hohnberger

It's About People
In what may be his most important book yet, Jim Hohnberger attempts to reconcile the faith we preach with the gospel we live—when we disagree. Jim shows how Jesus' attitude and approach towards those who didn't receive Him was just as important as the truth He taught.

0-8163-1964-2. Paperback.

US$10.99, Can$16.49.

Empowered Living
A thoughtful collection of principles and testimonies of how God can revolutionize your marriage, your family, and your walk with God.

0-8163-1917-0. Paperback.

US$14.99, Can$22.49.

Escape to God
How the Hohnberger family left the rat race behind to search for genuine spirituality and the simple life.

0-8163-1805-0. Paperback.

US$13.99, Can$20.99

New from Sally Hohnberger!

Parenting by the Spirit
Known for speaking on family issues in partnership with her husband Jim, Sally has put her experiences and the parenting techniques she has learned from her knees into print. The result is *Parenting by the Spirit*—a refreshingly practical and spiritual approach that helps you discover that your own vital connection with Jesus is the greatest secret to winning the hearts of your children.

If you've tried and failed to live up to your own and everybody else's unrealistic expectations and are willing to follow God's plan, this book will show you how to be the parent He designed you to be.

0-8163-2031-4. Paperback.

US$12.99, Can$19.49

Order from your ABC by calling **1-800-765-6955**, or get online and shop our virtual store at **www.AdventistBookCenter.com**.
- Read a chapter from your favorite book
- Order online
- Sign up for email notices on new products

For more information on the Hohnbergers' ministry or other materials, call 1-877-755-8300 or visit www.empoweredlivingministries.org.